Collins

Need to know?

Pensions

Collins

First published in 2006 by Collins
an imprint of
HarperCollins Publishers
77–85 Fulham Palace Road
London W6 8JB

www.collins.co.uk

A catalogue record for this book is available from
the British Library

Text: Helen Pridham
Editor: Grapevine Publishing Services
Designer: Judith Ash
Series design: Mark Thomson
Front cover photograph: Corbis
Back cover photographs: Corbis

ISBN 0-00-723466-X

Colour reproduction by Colourscan, Singapore
Printed and bound by Printing Express Ltd,
Hong Kong

Contents

Introduction

Most of us have a love-hate relationship with pensions. On the one hand, we would like the biggest pension we can get, preferably as soon as we can get it. On the other, we are easily put off serious pension planning – usually because we feel pensions are confusing or we are worried about getting ripped off.

The Government has recently announced its proposals for the future of pensions, including raising the state pension age to 68 and introducing a new national pension savings scheme. But if you want to decide your own retirement age and be sure of having enough retirement income, you still need to take control of your own pension planning. And do not delay because the later you leave it the more difficult it will get to save enough.

Costs on individual pensions have come down and they are more flexible than ever before. This means there are really no more excuses for delaying taking out or topping up a pension. This book will help you on your way. It covers all aspects of pensions, from state pensions to self-invested personal pensions. It also looks at the alternatives to pensions and what to do with your money when you get to retirement. Happy saving!

Acknowledgements

In writing this book I have received invaluable help from many people in the pensions world, to whom I am extremely grateful. Steve Bee at Scottish Life is a constant source of inspiration. Also, I would like to thank Lyn Webb and her colleagues at Legal & General, Ian Naismith at Scottish Widows, Justin Modray at Bestinvest and Robert Reid at Syndaxi, who so generously put their time and expertise at my disposal.

1 Why you need a pension

There are dozens of excuses to avoid or postpone taking out a pension, but even more reasons why they're a very good idea. This chapter is a general introduction to the benefits, along with analyses of the most common reasons why some people leave it until it's too late.

Why you need a pension

Pensions are in the news more than ever, yet most people are still confused by the subject. The way the state pension works remains a mystery to many, but there is a growing awareness that it won't be enough to provide a comfortable retirement.

must know

What is a pension?

A pension is basically a savings scheme with tax advantages. When you reach retirement, you can start drawing a regular income from your pension. This income usually comes from an annuity. The good thing about annuities is that they guarantee you an income for the rest of your life, unlike other types of savings and investments which can eventually run out.

Ask yourself these questions:
• Are you looking forward to retirement?
• Do you want to pursue your hobbies when you retire?
• Would you like to travel to exotic places when you stop working?
• Or even live abroad?
• Do you want to give younger relatives a financial helping hand when you retire?
• Do you know how much pension you will get at retirement?

If you have answered 'yes' to most of these questions but 'no' to the last, you have already made it clear why you need to think seriously about your pension. But if you are not convinced, this chapter will provide you with some more reasons why.

As we all know, there is much talk in the media and in Parliament of a pension 'crisis'. It sounds pretty dramatic. But what does it really mean? The main problem is that we are all living longer and as a result there are a growing number of retired people in the population. The number of workers relative to those in retirement is shrinking, which is making it more difficult for the state to afford adequate pensions. People have not been saving enough in their own private pension schemes to make up the difference. The Government has recently come up with some plans for solving this crisis, including raising the state pension age to 68, marginally increasing the basic state pension and introducing a new national pension savings scheme. But these plans will take some time to take effect and they will still not provide very generous pensions. Many people will want to retire earlier than 68. This means if you want to retire when you want on a decent pension, you will need to make sure you are saving enough yourself. These savings don't have to go into a pension plan. But a pension plan does have various advantages, as will be explained.

It is important not to rely on someone else to make sure you have enough retirement income. The Government's solutions will not provide the complete answer. Its track record so far has not been very good. When the current Government came to power it claimed that reform of pensions was one of its main priorities, yet it dilly-dallied and in some ways made things worse. The state pension system was made more complicated and means testing was introduced. Employers' pension schemes had to pay extra tax and cope with increased regulation. A positive step was the introduction of stakeholder pensions but these have not caught on in the way the Government hoped.

What can we do about it? If you want to take control of your own retirement, you should start saving for it without delay. 'But will my savings be safe?' you may ask. The unpredictable nature of shares and interest rates in recent years certainly seems to have made saving for retirement more

did you know?

In 1950, only one in ten of us was over 65. Now it is one in six. In another 30 years, over a quarter of the population will be 65 and over. Recent generations of parents have been having fewer children so in future there will be less people of working age paying tax towards pensions. At the same time people's health in later life has improved rapidly so we are living longer – which is good on the one hand, as it means we can all look forward to a longer and healthier retirement, but it also means there are more retired people in the population so the cost of providing state pensions will rise.

difficult. Yet over long periods the stockmarket has produced good returns and if you combine shares with other safer investments you can get the best of both worlds. We will be looking in more detail at how you can make the most of your retirement investments later in this book.

Why should I bother?

If you love your job so much that you want to go on working past age 65 – or whatever the state retirement age will be in years to come – then you may have a point. Why bother?

But even if you are keen to work, things may not always be that simple. Many employers are ageist, even though it is against the law, so getting or maintaining employment when you are older may not be easy. And even if finding a job isn't a problem, you may find that poor health or family commitments will put a stop to your plans.

Since you are reading this book, the chances are you feel you *should* bother with pension planning. Most people, no matter how much they like their job, would like to stop – or at least work part-time – when they get older so they have time to do things they didn't when they were working. If you can't enjoy life when you get to retirement, when can you? But you will need enough income.

A good pension will be your passport to fulfilling long-held ambitions such as travelling to far-flung places. When you only have a limited amount of annual holiday in a year, it hardly seems worth travelling anywhere too far away but when you retire, finding the time will not be a problem. You could even take the sort of 'gap year' that

must know

Six good reasons to have a pension

1. Because you would like to retire early if possible.
2. So you don't have to worry about how to pay the bills when you stop working.
3. So you can live it up a bit when you stop being a wage slave.
4. So you can travel more – go further afield and for longer.
5. So you can treat yourself and other people.
6.......................................

....

[add your own]

has become common among younger people having a break between school and university.

There are probably 101 other things you would like to do when you no longer have to earn a living. Pursuing hobbies such as gardening and golf remain perennially popular, but nowadays retired people are also taking up a whole range of activities from bungee-jumping to hang-gliding. You may want to do voluntary work or you may want to spend more time with your family, helping sons and daughters to do things they cannot fit in to their busy working lives.

What is so special about a pension?

A pension is nothing out of the ordinary. It really just acts as a tax-efficient 'wrapper' for your retirement savings. If you belong to a company pension, your savings will normally go into investments decided by those running the scheme, although you may be given a limited number of investment funds to choose from. If you have your own individual pension plan your range of investment choices may be much wider.

What makes pensions special compared to other ways of saving are the tax advantages they offer, and the fact that once you get to retirement they can provide you with an income for life no matter how long you live. Other forms of saving rarely offer this much certainty.

As for the tax advantages, there are three things to be aware of:
1) The best aspect of saving via a pension is the tax relief you get on your savings. This means more will go into your retirement pot than if you were saving elsewhere. Your savings are topped up with a tax

must know

Want to stop paying income tax?

Since April 2006, it has been possible to pay all of your annual salary into your pension and get tax relief on the whole amount (providing you don't earn more than the tax relief limit of £215,000, that is). If you did this you wouldn't be paying a penny in income tax because the taxman would have to give it all back to your pension provider. But this would only be possible, of course, if you had other money to live on.

refund from the taxman. So every £10 you save in your pension only actually costs you £7.80 with 22% tax relief added if you are a basic rate taxpayer, while higher rate taxpayers only pay £6 of their 'own' money.

2) The money you invest in your pension will grow virtually free of tax. There won't be any capital gains tax to pay on the investments in your pension pot, for example, whereas if you bought a buy-to-let property as a retirement investment you would face a capital gains tax bill when you sold it.

3) You can take 25% of your pension savings as a tax-free lump sum. At present you can do this at any time from age 50 but from 2010 the minimum age for taking money out of your pension will be 55. On the positive side, this means you won't be tempted to dip into your pension pot too early, as you might have been had you saved the money elsewhere.

Case study

Karl, 31, has been dithering about starting a pension for the last five years. Now he has been promoted and has decided to plough all of his £400 monthly pay rise into a pension. He is pleased by the fact that with basic rate tax relief his monthly savings will be worth £513 in his pension (i.e., £400 plus £113 tax relief) and that he won't be sharing any of his pay increase with the taxman.

So what's stopping you?

Most of us know we should be saving for retirement but it is easy to think of reasons for putting it off. This is one of the biggest mistakes you can make. Delays cost money when you are planning your retirement, however far off it might seem. If you catch yourself making one of the following excuses, think again. Set a deadline for sorting out your pension – and stick to it!

First excuse:
'I won't live that long.'
You might not. You could be hit by a bus tomorrow. But the chances are that you *will* live that long. People usually underestimate their life expectancy. Women in particular think they are going to die soner than they do. Research has found that women in their twenties underestimate their life expectancies by nearly nine years, while men in this age group underestimate their expected life span by around six years. Even women in their sixties think they are going to live four years less than they will on average.

Nowadays we are living longer than previous generations. This is why the Government is planning to gradually increase the state pension age to 68 by 2044. But even when it has been raised, pensioners will still be spending longer in retirement than our parents or grandparents.

In 1951 a man who reached age 65 could on average expect to live for another 12 years, while a woman of 65 could expect to live to age 81. In 2005, a man of 65 could expect to live another 19 years, while a woman's average life expectancy had increased to 87. This trend is continuing. By around 2050, the average man aged 65 is expected to live to 89, while a woman of 65 is expected to get past 90.

Improving life expectancies are not the only reason we are spending a lot longer in retirement. Over the years people have also been retiring earlier. In 1950, the average retirement age for men was 67, which meant they spent around 18% of their adult life in retirement. Women were also working longer. They retired at 64 on average and so spent some 26% of their life in retirement.

By 2005, men's average retirement age had fallen to 64. This meant the percentage of their adult life spent in retirement had increased to 31%, while women were retiring at 62 and consequently could expect to spend over 36% of their adult lives in retirement. Don't expect to die before you grow old!

How many more years will you live after 65?

Year you reach 65	Women	Men
2005	22.1yrs	19.4yrs
2015	23.0yrs	20.5yrs
2025	23.8yrs	21.3yrs
2035	24.7yrs	22.2yrs
2045	25.5yrs	23.1yrs
2054	26.3yrs	23.9yrs

Source: Government Actuaries Department

Second excuse:

'I don't want much, I'll manage on my state pension.'
The Government will pay you a basic state retirement pension providing you have made enough National Insurance contributions (See Chapter 2 for more details of how your state pension is calculated).

In 2006–07 the state pension for a single person is £84.25. You may also be eligible for a second state pension and you might be able to claim means-tested benefits to top up your weekly income.

The Government currently guarantees that no pensioner will have to live on less than £114.05 a week if they are single, while couples are guaranteed £174.05 a week. But will this really be enough for you to manage on?

Latest figures show that the average UK household spends an average of £434 per week. When you retire you will probably spend less on items such as transport as you won't have to travel to work each day. But even so official figures show an average single pensioner spends £133.40 a week. According to Age Concern, many pensioners feel they can only just cope. Do you really want to spend your final years watching every penny?

Third excuse:

'I have got a pension with my job – surely that's enough?'
A good pension with your job is worth its weight in gold, especially if it is a 'final salary' pension (which means you will get a fixed proportion of your salary when you eventually retire).

But many of the best company schemes have been closed because employers have found them too expensive to run due to poor investment markets, increased Government regulation and existing members living too long.

So if you are still in a company final-salary scheme you can usually count yourself lucky, providing you have belonged to it for long enough.

Case study

Jenny, 29, and her boyfriend Dave, 30, have just bought a flat together. Until now all her spare cash had been going towards building up the deposit for the flat. But she now wants to start saving for a pension before she settles down and has children. She knows she needs some spare cash in a savings account for emergencies but once she has put that money aside, she is going to put her spare cash into a pension. She decides to find out what type of scheme her employer offers.

Nowadays most employers are offering investment-linked schemes that do not provide a guaranteed amount of pension. Your retirement income will mainly depend on how much is in your pension pot when you stop work. There is nothing wrong with these so-called 'money purchase' pension schemes. The crucial question is how much is being paid into them. One of the problems is that companies do not tend to contribute very much to these schemes, if anything, so your pension may not be as big as you expect.

But for many people, the thing that most mucks up their pension planning is moving jobs. We tend to change jobs several times during our working lives nowadays, ending up with bits and pieces of pensions all over the place and no real idea of how much income they are going to provide us with in retirement. The only solution is to keep a regular check on what your different pensions are worth or possibly consider consolidating them in one place. (See Chapter 3 for more about your pension options when you change jobs.)

Don't be complacent. The chances are your work pension *will* need topping up

Fourth excuse:
'I can't afford to start saving for a pension.'
Fair enough. You have to live and if you have debts to repay, they should normally take priority over pension saving. But ask yourself – if you are having difficulty making ends meet now while you are working, how much more difficult will it be when all you have to live on is a limited pension?

Making modest savings now could make a huge difference to you in retirement. Even if you have other spending priorities at the moment, such as saving for the deposit on your first home, or for your children's education, bear in mind that it doesn't have to be all or nothing – it is often a good idea to split your savings between different goals.

You may actually be able to save more than you think if you take a long hard look at your finances to find ways of reducing your outgoings. Ask yourself if all your current spending is strictly necessary? Are there some treats that you could do without?

Waiting to start a pension until you feel you can afford it can actually make achieving your goal more difficult because it gets more expensive to make up for the time you have lost. The longer your money is invested the more time it has to grow.

---

did you know?

How current pensioners cope

40% of over 65s feel their social life is restricted by lack of money.
35% of over 65s cannot afford to spend a day out with friends or family.
33% of over 65s cannot afford to go out for a meal, enjoy a night at the pub with friends, or entertain friends or family at home.
29% of over 65s cannot afford to pursue a hobby or leisure activity.
41% of over 65s cannot afford a holiday.
Source: Age Concern, *Just Above the Breadline Report* 2006

The effects of delay are obvious if you consider the advice from pension experts about how much you should save in a pension. The rule of thumb is that if you want a pension that is equal to around two-thirds of your working income when you get to retirement (the level most people say they want), you need to save a proportion of your salary equal to half of your age when you start. So if you start saving at age 30, for example, you should put 15% of your earnings a year into your pension from then until you retire. But if you wait until age 40, you would need to save 20% of your earnings every year to make up for lost time, and at age 60, you have a problem.

You need to bear in mind, of course, that this rule of thumb will only provide you with a realistic pension if you are earning a reasonable amount when you start and your earnings remain relatively consistent. If you are currently working part-time or your earnings fluctuate a great deal you may need to save a higher proportion of your earnings to achieve your desired pension. (The next chapter deals in more detail with how you can work out how much you need to save).

Another good reason to start saving a modest amount regularly in a pension as soon as you can is that it gets you into the routine of saving. And once you set up a direct debit it gets easier to manage without that money. Get into the savings habit now!

Fifth excuse:
'My husband/wife has a good pension so I don't really need to bother.'
Many women rely on their husband's pension to provide for both of them in retirement. And there are

must know

How to top up a pension with 'free' money

You don't have to be a taxpayer to get basic rate tax relief on pension savings. If you are not working you can still pay up to £2,808 a year into a pension and get £792 of 'free' money added by the taxman. This is particularly useful if you want to keep up your pension contributions while you are taking a career break, say, to look after young children.
You can also set up pension schemes for children which will be topped by the taxman, giving them a head start in the retirement savings stakes.

probably some men who feel the same. So they see making contributions to their own pension as a lower priority. Even among those women who do have a pension, half stop saving for retirement when children come along.

Research by Scottish Widows shows that amongst men with children aged between 6 and 15, 40% are still saving in a pension, while less than half as many women with children in that age group – just 17% – are doing the same. If there is any extra cash available, men are more likely to save it while women tend to spend it on their children.

Women who rely on their husband's pensions are putting themselves in a risky position. For one thing, are they sure their husband is really saving enough to provide an adequate pension anyway? And then there is the possibility of family breakdown – one in two marriages nowadays ends in divorce.

Fortunately pensions are taken into account on divorce and they can be shared, so that the woman retains a proportion of her husband's pension when they split up (for more about this, see Chapter 6). But this may not be enough to provide either partner with a decent standard of living.

Women who live with a partner without getting married face an even more uncertain future. If the relationship breaks down or their partner dies, they have no legal right to a share in his pension.

Two pensions are better than one.

Sixth excuse:
'My house is my pension.'
Our homes tend to be our biggest investment and the enormous surge in house prices over the last

10 years has given many people the impression that they are sitting on a small fortune.

But it is important to be realistic about this investment. You will still need somewhere to live in retirement. You could trade down to a smaller property, releasing some of your capital to supplement your retirement income. But it's common for people to get very attached to their home as they get older and when it comes to it they don't want to move.

An alternative way of raising money from an existing property is through an 'equity release' scheme. These schemes will be discussed in Chapter 8 but they tend to be expensive and should only be regarded as a last resort.

Having a good pension means you won't be forced into moving or entering into deals that may eat up a large proportion of the value of your home.

Seventh excuse:
'I don't trust pension companies or financial salesmen.'
It is not surprising. There has been plenty of bad publicity about the pensions industry in recent years – pension mis-selling, rip-off charges, poor performance and Equitable Life going to the dogs. But government regulation has got much tighter to stop these problems recurring.

The Government's introduction of stakeholder pensions in 2001 has made a big difference to the cost of pensions. Stakeholder pensions are a low-cost, flexible, private pension. Charges are capped at 1.5% a year for the first ten years, reducing to 1% a year after that, and there are no penalties for stopping and starting savings or moving the money

must know

Does your partner's pension cover you?

If you and your partner are below pension age make sure you both let your pension trustees (the people responsible for your company pension scheme, or the pension provider if you have a stakeholder or personal pension) know that you want your partner to inherit your pension benefits. If your partner has already retired, he or she may have opted for a 'single life' pension, which would provide nothing for you on your partner's death. If you are not married or in a civil partnership you are unlikely to be entitled to any of your partner's pension if you split up. See chapter 6 for more on this.

to a new pension company. You can't go far wrong with a stakeholder pension.

The choice of investments you can put in pension plans has got wider, and these will be looked at in Chapter 5. You can now take out plans where you are not restricted to the investment funds run by the pension company itself. Funds run by other investment managers are also available, which should help to improve the return on your pension over the long term.

The best place to get advice about a pension is from an independent financial adviser and in Chapter 2 we explain how to find one. These advisers must give you the choice of paying a fee for their advice instead of automatically taking commission for selling you a pension. If you do opt for commission you have to be told exactly how much it is and how it compares with the amount other financial advisers are charging for the same service.

If you remain sceptical about pension companies and financial advisers, the best solution is to learn as much about pensions as you can so you know what is right for you. This way you can ask the right questions and judge for yourself the merits of what you are being offered and the advice you are given.

Learn to beat them at their own game.

Eighth excuse:
'I want to start a pension, but it's too confusing.'
If you feel like this, you are not alone. Just the word 'pension' can put some people off. But don't let it deter you from starting – or adding to – one of the most important investments you will ever make: your retirement savings.

Don't forget that at heart a pension is simply a method of building up a lump sum – with the help of the Government and maybe your employer – which you will be able to draw down when you stop working so you can enjoy your retirement to the full. The sooner you start your pension or sort out your existing pension pots, the easier it will be to achieve this goal.

In fact, pensions often appear more confusing than they actually are. This is partly because pension companies want to make their pensions sound enticing, with more features than their competitors, so they end up making them sound complicated. And as we know, the Government doesn't help much because state pensions are not the easiest of things to understand either.

However, progress is being made towards a simpler pension system. The Government introduced new rules in April 2006 lifting many of the restrictions on how much you can save in a pension and which types of pensions you can contribute to, which should help to make matters less complicated than they were in the past.

This book aims to clear up any confusion you may feel, answer all your pension questions and help you maximise your retirement income. After you have read it you should feel a lot more confident about your pension plans. Don't let yourself be bamboozled!

want to know more?

• If you consider yourself to be financially illiterate but know that you need to do some retirement planning, there's a quick and easy route you can follow. See the Pensions decision tree on pages 56-7 and read the explanation on pages 52-3, and that may be all you need for now.
• However, try to do the calculations of your current spending described in chapter 2. You'll find it an eye-opener.

weblink

• The government's Pension Service website at www.pension service.gov.uk has a wealth of useful information.

2 What to do next

Do you think that you will survive on the state pension supplemented by a couple of savings accounts here and there? Think again. In this chapter, you will calculate how much you would need in retirement to fund the lifestyle you want, and then how much retirement savings you have organised at the moment. If there's a difference, it will be up to you to plug it.

What to do next

Now you must work out what pension you already have and how much you will need when you retire. Most of us will get a pension from the state and may have some existing private pensions. But how much are they worth? And how can we boost them so we can look forward to getting the right amount of pension when we retire?

must know

Cutting back

Filling out a monthly spending form can be an interesting exercise on several fronts. Why not use it as an opportunity to see where you can make cutbacks – for example, saving on utility bills, mortgage, car insurance or home phone contracts? Spending a couple of hours phoning round or searching the internet for better deals could save you hundreds of pounds a year which you could then use to boost your pension savings. Useful websites are listed on page 20.

What do you know already?

Let's see how much you know about your pension first. Can you answer the following questions?
1. How much income do you think you will you need when you retire?
2. How much state pension will you get?
3. Could you improve your state pension?
4. Does your employer have a pension scheme?
5. How much should you save for your pension?
6. What will your current pension plans provide?

Don't worry if you answered 'don't know' to most of these questions. Few people would know all the answers. But filling the gaps in your pension knowledge will help you plan more effectively for the future, and this chapter will help you to do this.

Your retirement aims

One approach to pension planning is simply to save as much as you can afford. But this is a bit hit and miss. A better way is to work out how much income you think you will need when you retire and then draw up a savings plan that will meet your needs. A good way to start is to consider what you would like to do with your time when you stop working.

Are you someone who would like to retire at 55 to play golf on the Costa del Sol or travel to the Far East? Or would you be happy to work as long as you can and stay living near your family?

If you are intending to move or change your lifestyle you will need a lump sum when you retire. You may be planning to sell your current home and downsize to raise the money to pay for this but will it be enough? The tax-free cash you can take from your pension will provide you with more resources. And how much regular income will you need to cover your outgoings?

What's your current spending?

One of the best ways of working out how much income you are likely to need in retirement is to tot up your current spending. To do this it will help if you have a calculator, paper and pen, plus copies of the last full year's bank statements and credit and store card bills.

Use your bank statements and credit card bills to work out your current outgoings and fill in the left-hand column of the form on pages 28-9. It's best if you take an average over a year, thereby ironing out any extraordinary expenses. For quarterly bills, add four together and divide by 12. If your council tax is split over 10 months, add the 10 payments together and divide by 12. Count up the total you spent on holidays in the year and divide by 12. By the entry called 'Cash', include money you withdrew from cash machines (again, dividing the year's total by 12).

Now add up your current monthly spending. This can be a scary moment, especially if it comes to more than you earn, but everyone should do this

must know

Present and future

By the time you get to retirement age, your spending habits will probably have changed somewhat, but working out your current spending is a useful starting point. Few people know exactly where all their money is going each month.

2 What to do next

	Monthly spending	
	What you spend now	**Expenditure in retirement**
Home		
Mortgage or rent	£xxx	£xxx
Electricity	£	£
Gas	£	£
Water rates	£	£
Council tax	£	£
Buildings insurance	£	£
Contents insurance	£	£
Transport		
Car loan	£	£
Petrol	£	£
Car insurance	£	£
Road tax	£	£
Public transport	£	£
Taxis	£	£
Living expenses		
Food (supermarket bills, etc.)	£	£
Cleaning supplies	£	£
Toiletries	£	£
Laundry, dry cleaning	£	£
Medicines, medical costs	£	£
Other monthly bills		
Telephone (landline)	£	£
Telephone (mobile)	£	£
Internet connection	£	£
Child care	£	£
School fees/university costs	£	£
Children's clubs/lessons	£	£
Life assurance	£	£
Income protection insurance	£	£
Private health insurance	£	£
Alimony or child support	£	£
Pension	£	£
Endowments	£	£
Regular savings	£	£
Current debt repayments (e.g. bank loan)	£	£
Other (specify)	£	£

Entertainment

Meals in restaurants	£	£
Takeaways	£	£
Pub/off licence/wine bar	£	£
Tobacco	£	£
TV licence	£	£
Cost of TV digital channels	£	£
Books, magazines, newspapers	£	£
CDs, music	£	£
Tickets for cinema, concerts, sports, etc.	£	£
Sports/hobbies (inc. club memberships)	£	£
Children's activities	£	£
Lottery tickets, gambling	£	£
Home improvements	£	£
Gardening	£	£
Other (specify)	£	£

Irregular expenses

Home repairs	£	£
Appliances (new, repair etc.)	£	£
Car repairs	£	£
Pets (food, supplies, vet bills)	£	£
Holidays/travel	£	£
Christmas/seasonal gifts	£	£
Birthdays and non-seasonal gifts	£	£
Clothing	£	£
Children's toys	£	£
Hairdresser or barber	£	£
Other beauty treatments	£	£

Cash	£	£

Total spending per month	£	£

Capital expenditure plans for the future

New car	£	£
New property	£	£
Travel	£	£
Other	£	£

exercise from time to time to find out exactly where their money is going.

Now fill out the right-hand column of the form, trying to estimate the expenses you will have in retirement. If you have paid off your mortgage, there will be no more mortgage payments, and you might not need to spend so much on clothes or travel to work, but you may need extra cash for heating costs, paying others to do maintenance work or gardening you would have previously tackled yourself or to pursue new hobbies in your leisure time.

If you decide that you would like to move home when you retire, will you be able to sell your current property for enough to fund the move, or will you have additional expenses to cover? Be realistic, though. It's unlikely you'll save enough to buy your own South Sea island if you're currently earning £20,000 per annum and putting away £50 a month in a pension fund.

Add up the figures in the right-hand column to estimate the monthly income you would need in retirement. Most people say they would like to retire on a pension that's about two-thirds (66%) of their current income. The sad truth is that the average income of a single pensioner in the UK is currently just 44% of average earnings.

Don't forget about inflation

It's all very well working out how much income you would need if you were to retire tomorrow, but by the time you actually retire many of your monthly bills are likely to have increased due to inflation. Say you've worked out that you will need £1,000 a month to live on in your retirement: by the time you stop working maybe 10 years from now – even if inflation continues at its current low rate of around 2% – your £1,000 will only buy the equivalent of about £820 in today's money. In 20 years' time, it will only have the purchasing power of £670. This is because prices are rising by 2% a year, so the loaf of bread that costs £1 today will cost £1.22 in 10 years and £1.49 in 20 years, and all other goods will increase at around the same rate (some more, some less).

It's impossible to predict how much prices will rise between now and your retirement, but you cannot afford to ignore inflation when you are working out how much you need to save for the future. It's best to assume that prices will continue to rise at least as fast as they are now.

To get an idea of how much income you will need at different rates of inflation have a look at the inflation multiplier on page 32. If you plan to retire in 20 years and you think inflation will continue at 2%, the multiplier is 1.49. That means you should multiply the amount of retirement income you reckon you'll need at today's prices by 1.49. So if you think you need £1,000 a month, you will actually need £1,490 in 20 years in order to buy everything that £1,000 buys today.

Once you have worked out your target monthly income, the next step is to work out where you might get it from. There could be several sources, but let's start by finding out how much the government might contribute (and how much it might then take away again as income tax. Yes, in case you didn't realise, pensioners pay tax too.)

Case study

Colin has discovered that as a result of taking a three-month holiday between March and May three years ago when he was between jobs he has failed to clock up two full tax years of National Insurance contributions. Only complete tax years (6 April one year to 5 April the next) of contributions count towards a state pension. He decides it will be worth making voluntary contributions for those three months to ensure he has two more years towards his basic state pension.

Inflation multiplier

Years to retirement	Assumed inflation rate				
	2%	4%	6%	8%	10%
1	1.02	1.04	1.06	1.08	1.10
2	1.04	1.08	1.12	1.17	1.21
3	1.06	1.12	1.19	1.26	1.33
4	1.08	1.17	1.26	1.36	1.46
5	1.10	1.22	1.34	1.47	1.61
6	1.13	1.27	1.42	1.59	1.77
7	1.15	1.32	1.50	1.71	1.95
8	1.17	1.37	1.59	1.85	2.14
9	1.20	1.42	1.69	2.00	2.36
10	1.22	1.48	1.79	2.16	2.59
11	1.24	1.54	1.90	2.33	2.85
12	1.27	1.60	2.01	2.52	3.14
13	1.29	1.67	2.13	2.72	3.45
14	1.32	1.73	2.26	2.94	3.80
15	1.35	1.80	2.40	3.17	4.18
16	1.37	1.87	2.54	3.43	4.59
17	1.40	1.95	2.69	3.70	5.05
18	1.43	2.03	2.85	4.00	5.56
19	1.46	2.11	3.03	4.32	6.12
20	1.49	2.19	3.21	4.66	6.73
21	1.52	2.28	3.40	5.03	7.40
22	1.55	2.37	3.60	5.44	8.14
23	1.58	2.46	3.82	5.87	8.95
24	1.61	2.56	4.05	6.34	9.85
25	1.64	2.67	4.29	6.85	10.83
26	1.67	2.77	4.55	7.40	11.92
27	1.71	2.88	4.82	7.99	13.11
28	1.74	3.00	5.11	8.63	14.42
29	1.78	3.12	5.42	9.32	15.86
30	1.81	3.24	5.74	10.06	17.45
31	1.85	3.37	6.09	10.87	19.19
32	1.88	3.51	6.45	11.74	21.11
33	1.92	3.65	6.84	12.68	23.23
34	1.96	3.79	7.25	13.69	25.55
35	2.00	3.95	7.69	14.79	28.10
36	2.04	4.10	8.15	15.97	30.91
37	2.08	4.27	8.64	17.25	34.00
38	2.12	4.44	9.15	18.63	37.40
39	2.16	4.62	9.70	20.12	41.14
40	2.21	4.80	10.29	21.72	45.26

The state pension

Most of us will get some state pension, but not everybody gets the same – there are several different types of state pension. This makes it very difficult to work out for yourself exactly how much you can expect at retirement. Some parts of what you get depend on your National Insurance (NI) contribution record and others are means tested. It is important to understand what is available so you can maximise your state pension by, for example, topping up your NI contributions or claiming means-tested benefits. But even so, relying on the state alone will leave you struggling to make ends meet in retirement.

What the state provides

To get the full basic state pension, the current rule is that you must have paid full NI contributions for nine-tenths of your working life. If you are a man your working life is considered to run from age 16 to 65 = 49 years. This means you must have paid contributions for 44 of these years.

Women whose official state pension age is 60 must have paid contributions for 39 years. From 2010 the rules will change. The number of years required to qualify for a full basic state pension will be reduced to 30 for both sexes.

If you haven't paid enough full years' NI contributions (only complete tax years – 6 April one year to 5 April the next – count), you will get a reduced state pension. Under the present rules, you must have contributed for at least 10 years (women) and or 11 years (men) to get the minimum of 25% of the full amount. The full state pension in the 2006–07 tax year is £84.25 per week for a single person and

must know

Your pension age

If you want to know exactly when you will receive your state pension, go to the Pension Service website (www.pensionservice. gov.uk) and use the State Pension Age Calculator.

Not sure how much National Insurance you've paid?

You can apply for a forecast of your state pension from the Department of Work and Pensions by filling out a form BR19 (call 0845 300 0168 and they'll fill it in for you over the phone). Or you can print one from the internet or complete it on line through the Pension Service website (www.pensionservice .gov.uk). The forecast will tell you how much pension you have already built up and how much you can expect to receive in today's money if you continue to contribute. It will explain if there is anything you can do to improve your pension. If you qualify for any additional state pension this amount will also be shown.

£134.75 per week for a married couple or those in a civil partnership. If both partners have paid enough full contributions they will each be entitled to a single person's state pension.

What about gaps in your contribution record?
You may have periods when you did not pay contributions due to time spent in higher education or training, or if you worked incomplete tax years, or you have spent time abroad. If you have gaps in your record, you may be able to fill them by paying voluntary contributions. You can also do this from abroad. The current cost of these contributions in the 2006–07 tax year is £7.55 per week. But there is a time limit. You only have six years in which to pay missing contributions.

Voluntary contributions can be a good investment providing you can achieve at least 11 qualifying years. But if you are near pension age, check with the Pension Service (0845 606 0265) that paying voluntary contributions won't reduce any pension credit (see page 39) you get.

If you are a married woman you may find that you will be better off claiming on the basis of your husband's record. After 2010 husbands and civil partners will also be able to claim on the basis of their wives' or partners' contribution record if that produces a better state pension than their own contributions.

You do not need to pay voluntary contributions if you qualify for NI credits. Those who qualify include:
• Young people who stay at school or college between the ages of 16 and 18 (but credits are not given for time at university)

• Those registered as unemployed and actively seeking work.
• Those who are incapable of work due to illness or disability.
• Men of 60 and over who have stopped work, providing they live in the UK. From 2010 credits will also be given to women in this age group.

Are you a carer?

You will need fewer years of NI contributions to qualify for a full basic state pension if you have taken time off work to look after a child or someone who is sick or disabled, because you will normally qualify for Home Responsibilities Protection (HRP). (Note that HRP is due to change after 2010 to a system of pension credits.)

This protection of basic pension rights has been provided since April 1978 and is given automatically to anyone receiving child benefit for a child under 16 or Income Support to look after a sick or disabled person. You can also apply for it if you are a registered foster carer throughout a full tax year or looking after someone who is receiving Attendance Allowance or a similar benefit for at least 35 hours a week (to do so you will need form CF411, available from local DWP offices).

Since 2002, HRP has also been given for the State Second Pension, but in the case of those receiving child benefit it only applies until a child reaches age 6, unless the child is sick or disabled.

If you need to claim HRP, bear in mind there is a three-year time limit. So if you cared for someone in the 2003/04 tax year, the latest date you can apply for HRP is 5 April 2007. Married women or widows

must know

Time spent abroad

If you worked and paid social security contributions in a country that has reciprocal arrangements with the UK they will count towards your pension. For more details: if you are back in the UK contact the Pension Service (tel: 0845 606 0265). If you are still living abroad, visit HM Revenue & Customs web-based Centre for Non-residents (www.hrmc .gov.uk) or contact the Pension Service's International Pension Centre (tel: 0191 218 7777).

who have chosen to pay a reduced rate of NI contributions do not qualify for HRP.

How to boost your state pension

Paying voluntary National Insurance contributions is one way to boost your pension if you have gaps in your record. Alternatively, you could delay taking your state pension beyond normal retirement age. As long as you delay by at least a year, your pension will be increased by 10.4% for each year deferred. If you prefer, you can take the pension you did not receive as a lump sum with interest added at 2% above bank base rate. But bear in mind, as with your regular weekly or monthly pension payment, the lump sum will be liable to income tax.

There is no limit to how long you can put off taking your pension and you don't have to work during this time. If you die before you are able to claim the extra benefits, your widow, widower or civil partner will normally be able to inherit them and can also choose between an increased state pension to add to their own state pension or a lump sum.

Additional state pensions

You may qualify for an additional state pension. There have been three of these schemes in operation since the 1960s:

• Graduated Retirement Benefit

This scheme, which ran between 1961 and 1975, applied to employees earning more than around £9 a week. The benefits depend on how many 'units' you accumulated and their value when you retire. The maximum graduated retirement benefit for the 2006-07 tax year is £8.77 per week.

---

must know

Tax and pensions

When you are calculating how much your pensions will give you to live on in retirement, don't forget that pensioners have to pay tax. When you get to 65, the threshold is £7,280 [in 2006], so you pay no tax if your annual pension, including the state pension, is less than this, but you will be taxed at a rate of 10% on amounts over this, rising to 22% if you get over £9,431 and 40% if your pensions exceed £33,300.

• State Earnings Related Pension Scheme (SERPS)

If you were an employee between April 1978 and April 1988, you will probably have built up some SERPS pension. After 1988, it became possible for employees to opt out of this part of the state scheme and have a personal pension instead. Those who didn't opt out remained in the scheme until April 2002. SERPS pensions are based on your earnings during the time you were contributing. So the more you earned, the higher your pension will be.

• State Second Pension (S2P)

This scheme was introduced in 2002. It is very similar to SERPS. The amount you get is related to how much you have earned but it provides more generous benefits than SERPS for those on low or moderate earnings. Unlike SERPS, you can build up an entitlement to S2P if you are someone with a long-term disability which prevents you from working, or a carer who can claim Home Responsibilities Protection (HRP). However, if you are caring for children you will normally only receive HRP for S2P until your children are 6. Latest figures published by the Department of Work and Pensions in 2005 shows that the average amount of SERPs and State Second Pension received is £12.29 per week. From 2012, S2P will be gradually converted into a flat-rate benefit by 2030.

Should you be contracted out of additional state pensions?

Since 1988 it has been possible to opt out of additional state pensions and have part of your NI contributions invested in a private pension instead.

must know

Planning to retire abroad?

You can receive your UK state pension if you retire abroad but you will only get yearly inflation increases in your pension if you are in Europe or one of the other countries with which the UK has a special agreement. Countries with no special agreement include Australia and South Africa. For more information visit the Government's website www.direct.gov.uk or contact the Pensions Service.

Initially, the Government made it a very attractive option for younger people by offering incentive bonuses on top of the usual rebates. This meant there was a good prospect they would get a higher pension from a personal pension than from the additional state pension they were giving up.

Since then the Government has reduced the NI rebates substantially. Even the Financial Services Authority (FSA), the City watchdog, now believes people who are contracted out of S2P are likely to end up with a lower pension and it is advising people to reconsider their decision. Some pension companies have told their customers to opt back into the state scheme.

There are arguments for staying out of S2P. You can control where your money is invested and if you choose the right funds it is still possible you could end up with a better pension. Since April 2006 it has also been possible to take a tax-free lump sum from a contracted-out pension, which you can't get with a state pension. And you can take benefits from age 50 (55 from 2010), whereas with S2P you will have to wait until state pension age. There is also the possibility that future governments may reduce the value of S2P.

But for most people, it is better to be safe than sorry. You could end up significantly worse off with a private pension if the investment performance is poor than you would with an extra state pension which will be index-linked (i.e. linked to the cost of living or rising earnings in the future).

If you are currently contracted out of S2P and you want to opt back in tell your pension company and they will arrange it. If you are not sure whether you are contracted out or not, contact your pension company for details.

Pension credit

It has been obvious for some time that state pensions alone do not provide an adequate retirement income, and even people with a modest private pension or other savings they can draw on have found it difficult to get by. In 2003 the Government therefore introduced a special means-tested benefit known as the 'pension credit' for pensioners on low incomes.

The credit actually consists of two components which start at different ages. You may get a bit of both or only qualify for one depending on the amount of private pensions and savings you may have accumulated.

• The guarantee credit

At present you can start claiming this when you get to 60. It will provide you with an extra benefit on top of your state pension to ensure you have a guaranteed minimum income of at least £114.05 a week if you are single or £174.05 a week if you have a partner (in the 2006–07 tax year).

• The savings credit

If you or your partner are 65 or over and you have a small amount of extra income from private pensions or any other savings or investments, you may be eligible for the savings credit if your total income in the 2006–7 tax year is less than £159 a week if you are single, or £233 a week if you have a partner. The maximum savings credit in the 2006–07 tax year is £17.88 a week if you are single or £23.58 a week for couples.

must know

As retirement approaches

If you have only made modest savings towards your retirement, you need to think carefully about the best way of using your spare cash between now and stopping work. Putting more into your pension may not be the right thing to do if it is going to push your income just over the upper limit at which you will qualify for Pension Credit. For 2006-07 this is around £159 per week if you are single or £233 if you are a couple. Every £1 you get from a pension will count towards the limit. You may be better off using your money to clear any outstanding debts and then building up £6,000 of savings outside a pension as this will be excluded from the calculation of your means.

To find out whether you are eligible for Pension Credit you will have to be means-tested. So you will have to declare all your income, savings and investments. The first £6,000 of your savings will be ignored. But it will be assumed that every additional £500 you have is producing an income of £1 a week (even though in practice you may be receiving a much lower return).

Normally your entitlement to pension credits will be assessed shortly before you retire when your state pension is being calculated. If it isn't, or your circumstances change and you think you may be eligible, you can apply to the Pension Service either by phone (tel: 0800 99 1234) or by printing a form from their website and sending it to the address given. Claims can be backdated by up to 12 months.

Even if you think you will only get a very small amount of pension credit it is worth applying as it means you will also be able to claim Housing Benefit and Council Tax Benefit (help with your rent or mortgage and council tax, available from your local council).

The future value of state pensions

One of the major drawbacks of the basic state pension has been that its value in relation to what people are earning at work was gradually shrinking. Although it is increased each year in line with inflation – i.e., rising prices – earnings generally rise faster than prices so the state pension has become worth less and less relative to average earnings.

The Government has now agreed to link increases in the state pension to increases in average earnings. But this won't start until 2012. By then the basic pension will have shrunk to less than 14% of average earnings. After that it won't get any bigger in relation to earnings. It just won't get smaller. So if you want a larger pension relative to your pre-retirement earnings you will still need to make sure you save enough privately.

What other pensions do you have?

If you have never put money into an employer's pension or private pension and are about to start your retirement savings from scratch, you can skip this section. But if you have, you need to work out exactly what it will be worth when you retire so you know what the shortfall is, and how much more you need to save.

If you have worked for just one employer or saved in just one pension plan, it shouldn't be too difficult. But many people move

The shrinking basic state pension			
Tax year	Pension – weekly amount*	Weekly national average earnings*	Projected pension as a % of national average earnings
April 2006	£84.25	£541	15.6%
April 2007	£86.35	£565	15.3%
April 2008	£88.50	£591	15.0%
April 2009	£90.70	£618	14.7%
April 2010	£92.95	£646	14.4%
April 2011	£95.25	£675	14.1%
April 2012	£97.65	£706	13.8%

*Projected amounts after 2006   Source: Pensions Policy Institute

jobs every few years or start and stop pension plans, so they have small amounts of pension dotted around here and there and have little or no idea how much income they will eventually get at retirement.

Some years ago the Government proposed that all employees should be provided with 'composite pension statements' every year. It was intended that these statements would show you exactly how much pension you could expect from your company and personal pensions, past and present – as well as your state pension – all in one place. However, although some pilot projects have been undertaken, there is still no set date at which these combined statements are going to be available to all.

This means you will have to get the details together for yourself, or ask an independent financial adviser to help you.

In theory each of your pension providers should send you a statement every year telling you how much they are likely to pay you at retirement or how much your pension pot is likely to be worth. But in practice it doesn't always happen.

Case study

Kenny, 45, has worked out that he will need an annual income of around £20,000 in today's money when he retires. His state pension including his State Second Pension will be around £5,000 so he needs another £15,000 from a private pension. He thought he was on track to achieve this with the two pension plans in which he is currently saving but after checking his recent statements again and using the FSA's online pension calculator he realizes he needs to save another £100 per month. He is pleased he checked.

So here's what you need to do. Start by getting together any pensions paperwork you have. If you are lucky you will already have up-to-date statements with forecasts of how much pension you can expect and you can simply add them together with your state pension forecast (see box, p. 34) to work out what your total retirement income will be.

If you belong to a salary-based pension scheme (for more on how these work, see Chapter 3) your pension statement will usually show the pension you can expect at the company's normal retirement age. It will assume you continue to work for the company until you reach that age. The actual pension forecast will be based on your current salary so you will have a good idea of its present value. By the time you reach retirement you may be on a different salary – higher, it is hoped! – which will give you a different pension.

However, for investment-based pensions (also known as 'money purchase' pension schemes – for more on these see Chapter 3), you may find you have been sent several sets of figures for each pension, which can be rather confusing. By law, pension companies must nowadays give you a figure showing the 'buying power' of your annual pension at your selected retirement age. This figure assumes your pension savings continue to grow at 7% a year between now and retirement but is then reduced to take account of inflation. It can make your future pension look rather low!

In addition, though, you may be provided with details of your current fund value and a projection of your pension at your selected retirement age assuming two or three standard growth rates of 5%, 7% and 9% plus a standard annuity rate as laid down by the Financial Services Authority. A projection of your pension, with or without a lump sum, will normally also be given (this may or may not assume that you are going to pay further contributions into your pension).

What a personal pension statement may show*

Your fund value at the statement date		£3,600
The buying power of your projected annual pension in six years' time		£200

The projected benefits at your selected retirement date in six years' time:

	At 5% p.a. growth	At 9% p.a. growth
Your fund at age 60	£4,890	£6,390
Your annual pension	£248	£501
OR		
Your reduced annual pension	£186	£376
Plus tax-free lump sum	£1,220	£1,590

* For someone six years away from retirement

You will probably find it easier to base your planning on pensions projections in today's money. But always bear in mind the impact of inflation.

Some pension providers may only give you the current lump sum value of your pension pot ('your fund value at statement date'). This is typically the case if you have an old-style 'retirement annuity' pension taken out before 1 July 1988 (when they were replaced by personal pensions). If so, you will need to convert that amount into a potential pension. You can do this using the official pension calculator website of the Financial Services Authority (FSA) at www.pensioncalculator.org.uk. Or for a rougher rule of thumb you could look at current annuity rates shown in the money pages in much of the weekend press. The tables in the money pages of newspapers usually show how much income can be purchased with a pension fund of, say, £10,000, so you will probably need to do a bit of maths depending on the actual size of your pension pot (for example, if your fund is worth £15,000 you multiply the figure by 1.5).

When you have totalled up how much income you can expect, you can then compare that figure with the income you worked out you would require at the beginning of this chapter.

If you don't have up-to-date statements or can't find them, you will need to ask all of your pension providers for new projections. Contact human resources departments for details of your company pensions and customer service departments for personal pension plan, stakeholder pension and retirement annuity figures.

If you have to write to your pension providers to ask for projections use the opportunity to ask for other information about your policy at the same time, such as the type of plan, where it is invested and so on. (See page 46 for a list of questions you

must know

What is an annuity?

An annuity is an investment product you buy at retirement with your pension lump sum in order to provide your regular pension income for the rest of your life.

might want to ask. Don't worry if you don't understand some of the terms just now – all will be explained in later chapters.) This will help you to review and check your policies to make sure they are up to scratch. If you can't find your policy number or membership number, give your National Insurance number and date of birth so your pension providers can find you on their records.

Future developments

Having to chase around after all your pension providers to get comparable figures is a time-consuming but worthwhile exercise. In the future it may become much easier. The Department of Work and Pensions (DWP) is intending to introduce an internet-based 'pension planner' which will enable people to get details of the likely retirement income from all their pension plans in one place at the click of a mouse. The DWP is planning to start a pilot exercise with some pension providers in 2006 but could eventually make it compulsory for all pension companies to provide details for their customers through this website.

If you have lost touch with past employers or pension companies that have since changed their names, you will need to do some detective work. Fortunately, the Pension Tracing Service can often provide you with contact details. You can request information online through the Pension Service

must know

Tracking down old pensions

The Pensions Tracing Service has a database of over 200,000 occupational and personal pension schemes and can be used to search for a scheme free of charge. It can be contacted through the Pension Service (www.thepen sionservice.gov). Alternatively, if you want someone else to carry out the search you could contact the Unclaimed Assets Register at www.uar .co.uk or tel: 0870 241 1713. According to the UAR, there is some £3bn in unclaimed pensions, and it professes to help even if you can only vaguely recall that you had a pension and have lost the paperwork, or are bereaved and think your partner may have had a pension. Each search costs £18 – but it could well be worth it.

What to write to your personal pensions provider

Customer Service Department   Policy Number:

Any Pension Company   Date of Birth:

Sometown PP1 1PP   NI Number:

Dear Sir/Madam,

Please supply me with the following details about my pension.

1 Type of plan:

2 Date started:

3 Selected retirement date:

4 Confirm total premiums paid to the plan

5 State in which funds the plan is invested

6 Supply an up-to-date performance bulletin and fund switch forms

7 Current value of the plan

8 Current transfer value of the plan

9 Please give current death benefit of the plan and state whether the policy is written in an individual trust

10 Are there any guaranteed annuity rates under the plan?

11 If yes, at what age and in what format?

12 Please supply full details of the charging structure of the plan, including any charges/loss of loyalty benefits on transfer, early or late retirement

13 Please supply projected maximum lump sum and pension at age .... [add the age at which you expect to retire].

14 Please state whether projection is based on the current value of the plan, or assumes payment of future premiums – if so, is it assumed that the premiums remain level or increase?

Yours faithfully,

website or tel: 0845 6002 537. The more information you give
the tracing service the better chance you have of success.
Details such as the name and address of your past employer,
its business, the type of pension scheme you belonged to,
and the name of the insurance company, if relevant, will all
help with the search.

Working out how much more you need to save

Now you can do the sums. In the table below, enter your
estimated monthly spending and the capital you will need at
retirement and then put in your state pension forecast and the
projected income and lump sums you can expect to receive
from any existing pensions. Subtract the second figures from
the first to find out precisely how much extra pension and lump
sum you will need.

		Monthly amount	Lump sum
A) Estimated spending in retirement		£	£
State pension forecast		£	£
Private pensions	1)	£	£
	2)	£	£
	3)	£	£
B) Total		£	£
A) £ , £ –			
B) £ , £			
= £ , £			

The amount you need to save to achieve these goals will depend
to a large extent on your age now and when you plan to retire.
The younger you are and the later you intend to retire, the less
you will have to save per month.

   The table on page 48 will act as a guideline as to how much
you should save. For a more specific figure go to the FSA's
official pension calculator at www.pensioncalculator.org.uk
or ask an independent financial adviser.

How much pension for your money?

Table shows projected annual pension and tax-free cash (TFC) at retirement age 65 based on different levels of saving per month by males and females of different starting ages

	Male aged 25	Male aged 35	Male aged 45	Male aged 55
£100 per month	£10,200 pa	£5,170 pa	£2,400 pa	£869.00 pa
	TFC £49,300	TFC £24,700	TFC £11,300	TFC £4,050
£250 per month	£25,900 pa	£13,100 pa	£6,070 pa	£2,180 pa
	TFC £125,000	TFC £62,700	TFC £28,700	TFC £10,100
£500 per month	£52,400 pa	£26,500 pa	£12,200 pa	£4,390 pa
	TFC £252,000	TFC £126,000	TFC £57,900	TFC £20,400
	Female aged 25	**Female aged 35**	**Female aged 45**	**Female aged 55**
£100 per month	£9,620 pa	£4,860 pa	£2,250 pa	£813.00 pa
	TFC £49,300	TFC £24,700	TFC £11,300	TFC £4,050
£250 per month	£24,400 pa	£12,300 pa	£5,700 pa	£2,040 pa
	TFC £125,000	TFC £62,700	TFC £28,700	TFC £10,100
£500 per month	£49,300 pa	£24,900 pa	£11,400 pa	£4,110 pa
	TFC £252,000	TFC £126,000	TFC £57,900	TFC £20,400

Figures assume a standard growth rate of 7% per annum and pensions are level annuities, guaranteed 5 years, payable monthly in arrears.

Source: Legal & General

Keeping an eye on things

Remember: once you have worked out how much you need to save, you must keep the figure under regular review to make sure you are still saving enough. Many savers go on putting the same amount into their pension year after year, even though their income – and spending – has risen.

One way of guarding against this gradual erosion in the value of your savings is to choose a pension where your pension company automatically increases the amount it takes out of your salary or from your bank account by a fixed percentage each year. Alternatively, it is often helpful to work out what you save as a proportion of your income. So if you are saving say £200 a month to achieve your retirement income goal and your monthly earnings are £2,000, this would mean you were saving 10% of your income. If you stick to this percentage as your income increases, this will help to ensure that your savings stay on track.

If you are starting your pension from scratch, one of the simplest yardsticks for working out how much to save to achieve a decent pension is to take your age and divide it in half to find out the percentage of your income you should be saving during the whole of your working life. This means 20-year-olds should save 10% of their income, 30-year-olds should save 15%, 40-year-olds should save 20%, and so on. Unfortunately, there is no easy rule of thumb for those who already have bits and pieces of pensions or who take career breaks. You really do have to do the sums.

want to know more?

• **The Financial Services Authority is a government-backed organisation designed to regulate financial service providers and protect consumers' rights. It also provides advice leaflets on a wide range of financial topics and comparative tables to help you find the best deals, although it won't recommend individual products. For its consumer helpline, tel. 0845 606 1234.**
• **If you have worked out how much pension you need, chapter 3 explains how to choose the best product to suit your requirements.**
• **To find out about your state pension entitlement, call the Dept. of Work and Pensions on 0845 300 0168.**

weblinks

• **www.fsa.gov.uk/ consumer**
• **www.thepension service.gov.uk**

3 Your pension choices

You've worked out how much you need to save and now you have to decide the kind of pension that makes most sense in your circumstances: salary-related or money purchase, stakeholder or personal, SIPP or GPP? Do you need to top up or transfer a pension? This chapter tells you how.

Your pension choices

Pensions come in different shapes and sizes. Some are run by employers, others you take out directly with a pension company. If you don't already have a pension, which should you choose? There are two ways of dealing with this question, depending on how much you want to know about the subject.

must know

Getting started

See the Financial Services Authority's (FSA) factsheet: 'FSA guide to pensions 1: Starting a pension', available from its website www.fsa .gov.uk/consumer or tel: 0845 606 1234.

The basics

• If you are an employee, your easiest option is to start saving into whatever pension you are offered with your job. If you are lucky your employer will also chip in. In fact, if your employer is prepared to pay into a pension for you, it is virtually a no-brainer. Go for it!

• Most employers are legally obliged to offer some kind of pension, so if you don't remember yours offering you one, ask!

• How much pension will you get? Most pensions now are so-called 'money purchase' schemes or – to put it in a nutshell – the more you put in the more you get out. But sometimes job-based pension schemes will give you a pension that is linked to how much you earn.

• You will have to take the initiative yourself if you are self-employed or you work for a very small company. You should probably take out a stake-holder pension – these are basic, low-cost pension savings plans.

• With which pension company? You generally won't go too far wrong if you choose a plan with one of the big insurance companies such as Legal & General, Prudential or Scottish Widows. The charges on stakeholder pension plans are laid down by the Government so there is not much to choose between these companies.

It can be as simple as that (and if you want a simpler version, see the decision tree on pages 56-7).

If you'd rather not know any more, you can skip to the next chapter. But if you are interested in the ins and outs of different pension plans, read on. You will have to be prepared for some jargon, but it will be to your advantage and help you understand and plan your pensions better – we can spell it out as we go along. But first try this little quiz.

Test your pension knowledge

1) Does your employer have to put money into your pension?

2) Name two types of company pension scheme.

3) What does AVC stand for?

4) What is the difference between a personal pension and a stakeholder pension?

5) What is a SIPP?

6) How much can you save in a pension each year?

If you're stumped by some of these but still curious, all will be revealed.

How much can you save?

There are basically two different types of pension – 'salary-based' and 'money purchase' (investment-based) – but they come in several different 'wrappers'. Some pensions are 'occupational' (job-related) schemes run by employers. Others are schemes for individuals run by pension companies. Nowadays you are not restricted to any one type of scheme. You can save in several different ones at the same time.

Since April 2006 the rules on how much you can save in a pension each year have become much more flexible. You can now get tax relief on savings of up to 100% of your earnings, or taxable profits if you are self-employed. At the very minimum everyone can pay £3,600 a year into a pension.

Maximum pension allowance		
Tax Year	Annual savings limit	Lifetime fund limit
2006/07	£215,000	£1,500,000
2007/08	£225,000	£1,600,000
2008/09	£235,000	£1,650,000
2009/10	£245,000	£1,750,000
2010/11	£255,000	£1,800,000

There are some restrictions. There is an upper limit on the annual amounts qualifying for tax relief that can go into a pension and there is also a maximum lifetime pension 'pot' that you can build up tax-free. But both limits increase every year and they are so high that they are unlikely to affect many people. Most of us are unlikely to save anywhere near the lifetime limit, but if you do, your savings will be taxed at 25% if you take them as pension when you retire, and at a whopping 55% if you take them as cash. If you are lucky enough to already have a pension fund around the lifetime limit, you may be able to protect it from extra tax if you register with HM Revenue & Customs by 5 April 2009. Seek independent financial advice first.

'I don't know how much my pension is worth at the moment.'

If you have a money purchase pension, it's relatively easy to work it out – it's the value of your pension fund built up from your savings, tax relief and investment growth. This will be shown on your pension statement. With final salary pensions, you multiply the pension you have built up by 20. So if you've built up, say, a £5,000 a year pension, it will be worth £100,000 in terms of the lifetime limit.

Your pension options: employer pension schemes

If your employer invites you to join a pension scheme run by the company – an 'occupational pension scheme' – you should normally agree. The good thing about being a member of this type of pension scheme is that your employer will put money into the pension on your behalf in addition to whatever you pay in. Not becoming a member means you will miss out on these employer contributions – you will be effectively turning down part of your salary and reducing your eventual pension.

Employers' pension schemes have traditionally fallen into two categories – salary based or money purchase. They have often provided extra benefits such as a spouse's or civil partner's pension if you die and free life assurance of up to four times your annual salary.

Salary-related pensions

Salary-related pension schemes (you may also hear them referred to as 'defined benefit' schemes) aim to provide you with a pension linked to the size of your salary. Traditionally, the pension was related to your salary in the final years of your working life prior to retirement, which is why they are often described as final salary pension schemes. But a growing number of the remaining schemes are switching to 'career average' pensions where your pension is linked to your average salary during the whole of your working life with a company.

You will normally be required to contribute to the cost of the scheme. The typical employee contribution in the past was

Pension decision tree

Are you working?

Yes

Do you work for an employer?

Yes

Does your employer offer an occupational pension scheme that you are eligible to join?

Yes

Join your company pension scheme. Your employer will make contributions on your behalf, so it is usually the best way to save for retirement. You can top it up with a stakeholder pension, personal pension or other savings, if need be.

Yes

This may have better terms than a personal pension you could arrange on your own, especially as your employer will have to make contributions on your behalf.

Yes

If your employer will make contributions to it it is worth joining their scheme. If not, compare the terms with others you find through your own research.

No

You can contribute up to £3600 a year to a stakeholder pension, or get someone to do this on your behalf. You can also start your own personal pension scheme or invest in ISAs. But you may not be building any entitlement to a state pension. It might be wise to pay voluntary national insurance contributions.

No

If you are self-employed, you can choose from a stakeholder pension or a personal pension scheme. Keep up your national insurance contributions to earn your entitlement to a full state pension.

No

Does your employer offer you a group personal pension scheme?

No

Does your employer offer a stakeholder pension? By law, most do.

No

You will need to make your own retirement income provisions, either with a stakeholder pension or a personal pension scheme.

around 5% of salary but this has increased in recent years. Your employer is expected to pay the rest. Both your contributions and your employers' are normally put into a pension fund that holds a variety of investments, unless you work in the public sector (i.e., for the Government), where pensions are not pre-funded.

Salary-related pension schemes are considered the best type of scheme for employees because they provide a predictable amount of pension. But they have become a dying breed. Until the mid 1990s, the majority of large employers offered final salary schemes. But the costs of these schemes have rocketed in recent years. A major problem was caused by the slump in the stockmarket between 2000 and 2003, which sent the value of pension funds tumbling. This setback has been combined with ex-employees living longer, resulting in more being paid out in pensions. In addition there are new Government rules about how pension funds should invest their money.

All these things have meant that many salary-based pension schemes are in 'deficit' and have less money in the kitty than they need to meet their obligations. As a consequence, employers are often having to pay large amounts into their pension schemes to make up the deficit and many companies have decided to close their salary-based pension schemes to new employees. Some have also closed them to existing employees, and many of those that remain open are being modified. Employees are being asked to contribute more and pension ages are being raised. The basis on which future pension benefits are calculated is also being changed. The main place where final salary schemes can still be found nowadays is in the public sector.

How your pension is calculated in a salary-based scheme
In a salary-based scheme, the size of your pension will depend on how long you have been a member of the scheme and how much you earn.

For each year you belong to the scheme you will normally build up or 'accrue' either one sixtieth or one eightieth of your salary towards your pension. So if you contribute to the scheme for twenty years, for example, you could have a pension of say 20/60ths or one third of your salary.

Even if your scheme is still final salary-based, it may not necessarily be linked to your salary in the year you leave. Definitions vary. It could, for example, be the average of your last three years' salary. Nowadays, to bring down costs down, some pensions are being linked to your 'career average' salary, taking your average salary for your whole period of employment. Once you start receiving your pension it will be increased each year in line with inflation.

How healthy is your employer's pension scheme?

Many private company salary-based pension schemes are in 'deficit', which means they have less money in their fund than they need to pay all the pensions they have promised. If you want to know whether yours is in this position, ask your human resources department how to contact the pension administrators and ask them. If it is in deficit it doesn't mean you have to worry. The Pensions Regulator is currently working with companies to ensure they top up their schemes. For more details, see Chapter 7. If you are worried about your pension scheme, contact the Pensions Advisory Service for free advice (tel: 0845 601 2923).

Money-purchase schemes

The majority of employers' pension schemes open to new employees nowadays are investment-based money purchase schemes (sometimes also referred to as 'defined contribution schemes'). Employees are usually required to pay around 3% of their salaries into these schemes and employers pay in a similar amount. Some companies give employees the option of paying in larger amounts and will then match these additional contributions, so if the employee puts in, say, an extra 2%, the employer will add another 2%.

The money you and your employer contribute to the scheme may go into a managed investment fund which will be put into a variety of different investments, including UK and overseas shares, government and corporate bonds, commercial property such as offices and shops, and cash deposits. Or you may be given a choice of investment funds – see Chapter 4 for details of the different types of funds that you may be offered.

The main feature of this type of pension scheme is that you will have your own pension pot, a defined amount of money consisting of the contributions plus tax relief and the growth in the investments, which you can use to purchase a regular pension income in retirement.

How your pension is calculated in a money-purchase scheme

As the name suggests, the amount of pension you will get from this type of scheme will largely depend on how much money you have in your pension pot when you stop working. The more you have put in, the more you will get out. Although it is no longer compulsory to buy a pension annuity at retirement most of us will need to do so to get a reliable pension.

The amount of income you get from an annuity depends on a number of factors (for more on annuities see Chapter 5) but two of the biggest influences are the general level of interest rates at the time you retire and the type of annuity you decide to buy. When your scheme buys the annuity on your behalf it will normally buy one that increases in line with rising prices and provides a pension for a partner should you die first. But if you prefer you can decide on the type of annuity you want to buy under the open market option.

Generally the amount of pension you will get from a money-purchase pension will be less than you will get from a salary-based pension. The main reason is that employers tend to put much lower contributions into these schemes. If more were paid in, more pension would be paid out.

What happens to your occupational pension when you change your job?

When you change jobs, leaving an occupational pension scheme behind you, you will have a number of options as far as your pension is concerned, which are outlined below. They will partly depend on how long you have been a member of the scheme. If you have been in a scheme for more than two years, you will be able to choose from the three options explained below. If it is less than two years, your options will be slightly different. You won't normally be able to leave your pension where it is. You will have to decide between transferring it to a new pension scheme (options 2 and 3) or taking a refund of your contributions. Getting cash back may sound attractive but it is rarely a good idea and people who

did you know?

Annuity companies make calculations based on average life expectancies in the UK, which are rising all the time. In 2005, men aged 65 could expect to live to the age of 84 and women of 65 would live to an average of 87. Women get lower annuity rates because of their higher life expectancy.

go for this option usually regret it later when they realise they haven't saved enough for their retirement.

must know

Worried about security?

Over the last few years there has been a number of reports of companies that have gone bust, leaving their salary-related pension schemes 'in the red'. Employees have not only lost their jobs but much of their retirement savings as well. To save other employees from this fate, the Government set up the Pension Protection Fund in April 2005. If a company becomes insolvent now, the fund will provide you with a replacement pension. For more details of the Pension Protection Fund see Chapter 7, or go to the website www.pension protectionfund.org.uk.

The three options normally available when you change jobs are:

1) To leave your pension where it is. You can simply leave your pension in your old employer's scheme until you retire. If it is a salary-related scheme, your pension will be based on your salary at the time you leave but it will be increased in line with rising prices up to a maximum of 5%. However, since earnings tend to rise faster than prices, its value compared to what you are earning when you finally retire may have fallen considerably. If you belong to a money purchase scheme, your money will remain invested so its value at retirement will depend on investment performance.

2) Transfer your pension to your next employer's scheme. You can take a transfer value from your old scheme and put it into your new employer's scheme. However, unless you are transferring within the public sector, taking salary-related benefits to a new employer's scheme can be difficult if not impossible nowadays. Your new employer's scheme is not obliged to accept your transfer value and as most schemes are now closed to new employees, they may well refuse. The other problem is that if your last scheme was 'in deficit' your transfer value will also be reduced accordingly (as explained in the next section).

Transferring between money-purchase pension schemes is easier – you can just take your pension pot from one scheme to the next. What you need to do in this situation is compare the investment performance and charges of the two pension providers before deciding whether to transfer.

3) Transfer your pension to a stakeholder pension or personal pension scheme or Section 32 Buyout Bond (see box, right). You could take your transfer value from your old employer's scheme and invest it in your own stakeholder pension or personal pension scheme – how these work and the differences between them are discussed over the next few pages. You can then add to the fund yourself and control the investments. A buyout bond could be used if part of your transfer value includes a guaranteed minimum pension, but you won't be able to make further contributions.

Which option is best for you?

You will need to weigh up a number of pros and cons. If your old pension scheme was a salary-related scheme in deficit – that is, the value of its investments is lower than the amount of pensions it owes to members – your transfer value will be reduced accordingly. In other words, if there is, say, a 25% deficit you will only get 75% of the true worth of your pension as a transfer value.

If your ex-employer's business is sound it may be better to wait until the shortfall has been made up. The Pensions Regulator is working with employers to make sure they put enough in their pension funds to meet their obligations. And if the worst comes to the worst and your former employer goes bust there is the Pension Protection Fund, which will give you 90% of your pension if you have not yet reached retirement age and 100% if you have

must know

What is a Section 32 buyout bond?

These bonds are sold by insurance companies. Your money is put into investments so it is like a personal pension but if part of your old pension was guaranteed, a buyout bond will preserve that guarantee. If you want to know whether part of your pension is guaranteed, ask your pension administrators. Seek independent financial advice on whether you should transfer to a buyout bond or not.

must know

Questions to ask prospective employers about their pension scheme

1. Find out if it is salary-related or a money-purchase scheme, or is it a stakeholder or personal pension arrangement?
2. Ask how much your employer will contribute on your behalf.
3. For a salary-related scheme, ask if it is linked to final or average salary and what fraction of salary is earned for each year of contributions (for example, one sixtieth).
4. If the scheme is not run by the company, which pension provider is it with?
5. For non-salary-related schemes, ask about your investment choices.
6. Are any other benefits provided, such as life insurance?

already retired. The maximum pension covered by the Fund is £25,000 at age 65. If your pension higher, you may feel the protection offered by the Fund is not enough. You may believe you could do better investing the money elsewhere. This is a difficult decision and you will need to take independent financial advice.

Transferring between two money purchase occupational schemes is more straightforward but it is still a good idea to take professional advice to help you compare charges and investment performance.

Transferring from an occupational scheme to a stakeholder pension or personal pension scheme needs very careful consideration. You will need to take into account any guarantees and benefits you may be giving up. Transferring from a salary-related scheme to a stakeholder pension or personal pension means you will be giving up a secure pension and taking on the investment risk yourself. Despite the risks, some people may prefer having greater control over their investments. Always take independent financial advice before transferring.

Other schemes you may be offered by an employer

If your employer has five or more employees, you must be offered access to some form of pension. If your employer does not provide an occupational scheme that you can join, you must be offered either a group personal pension or a stakeholder pension.

Stakeholder pensions

The Government introduced stakeholder pensions in April 2001. Stakeholder pensions are basically low-cost, flexible retirement savings plans run by insurance companies. One of their most reassuring features is low charges. Until they were introduced, the charges on personal pensions had been high and often deliberately confusing. With stakeholder pensions, your annual charge must not exceed 1.5% of the value of your pension for the first 10 years and 1% thereafter. Some pension companies charge less. Any additional charges must be optional.

The other attractive points about stakeholder pensions are the low minimum investments, the ability to stop and re-start contributions without penalty and the lack of penalties if you want to transfer your money elsewhere to a different pension provider.

Here are some points to note about stakeholder pensions and your job:

• Although your employer is legally obliged to offer you access to a stakeholder pension if the company has five or more staff, this may simply involve giving you the details of a designated pension company when you first join the company. If you can't remember being offered a scheme, ask your employer for details.

• Your employer is not obliged to pay anything into a stakeholder pension on your behalf. But some employers do and if yours does, it makes sense to join it otherwise you will be missing out on a valuable contribution towards your retirement savings. If not, it may still be a good idea to join the scheme your employer has nominated, as it will save you the hassle of finding one.

• If you decide to save in the stakeholder pension designated by your employer, you can ask for your pension savings to be deducted automatically from

must know

Becoming a trustee of your company scheme

Company pension schemes are required to have some employees of the company on the board of trustees. If you want to know more about how your pension scheme is managed, why not volunteer for this role?

your salary and passed to the pension company. If you find saving difficult, this is a good way of ensuring you are not tempted to spend the money on something else. You can ask for a flat amount, say £100 a month, or a set percentage of your pay, say 10%, to be deducted and paid into your pension. You can change the amount at six monthly intervals. The minimum contribution is £20 a month.

• On top of the amount you pay into a stakeholder pension, tax is reclaimed from the taxman by your pension company and also invested in your pension. Higher-rate taxpayers have to claim their extra relief through their tax return.

• A stakeholder pension will normally offer you a choice of investment funds. If you don't want to make the choice, don't worry. There will be a perfectly good 'default' option, normally a 'lifestyle' fund. These are funds where your contributions are invested in shares initially but are later switched into safer fixed interest investments as you get near to retirement age. (For more on other investment options in stakeholder pensions see Chapter 4.)

• A stakeholder pension is a contract between you and your pension provider. So your employers have no say over your pension, even if they are making a contribution.

Case study

When Sandra, 28, first joined her company a year ago she was offered a stakeholder pension. But she turned it down because she didn't think she could afford it even though her employer was prepared to contribute 2% of her salary to the scheme if she joined. Now she realises she has been missing out on £40 a month from her employer towards her pension and has decided to start contributing herself.

Group personal pensions

Some employers offer group personal pensions instead of stakeholder pension schemes. These arrangements often date from before stakeholder pensions were introduced. They work on very similar lines. The main difference is that personal pensions are not subject to the same cost controls as stakeholder pensions so it is wise to check what the annual charges amount to.

But even if they are slightly more expensive (the annual management charge may be over the maximum 1.5% a year limit on stakeholder pensions), the advantage of being offered a group personal pension is that your employers are legally obliged to put money into this type of pension for you. They have to pay in an amount equal to 3% of your salary, on top of whatever you save. So you would be unwise to turn down the offer of joining such a scheme and miss out on that payment from your employer.

As with stakeholder schemes, your personal pension is an individual contract between you and your pension provider. Your employers have no control over your pension even though they are making a contribution.

How much pension will you get from a stakeholder pension or personal pension?

The size of pension you will get from stakeholder pensions and personal pensions will depend on two main things:

1) How much is in your pension pot when you get to retirement – this will depend on how much you have saved and how well your investments have performed.

2) Pension annuity rates – Although it is no longer compulsory to buy an annuity at retirement, most people need to do so to provide themselves with a regular pension. One of the main influences on annuity rates is the general level of interest rates. (For more on annuities, see Chapter 5.)

What happens when you leave an employer stakeholder pension or group personal pension?

One of the good things about stakeholder pension and group personal pension plans is that they are much simpler to deal with when you move employers. As they are individual contracts between you and the pension company, you have full ownership and control and can take your plan with you. Some things may change, though. If your ex-employer has previously paid money into the plan on your behalf this will obviously stop. Also if your employer has subsidised the charges, these may rise when you leave the company. You will then have a number of choices about what to do with your plan.

• You could decide to stop paying into it. Your money can then remain invested with that pension company until you decide to retire and draw the benefits.

• You can continue paying into it. But find out if your new company offers a stakeholder pension or group personal pension you can join. You could contribute to both, but if your budget is limited this may not be possible. If your new employer offers to put money into its designated pension if you join, then you would be better off paying into that one. You may find your new employer's scheme also offers better investment choices or has lower charges.

• If your new employer offers a stakeholder or group personal pension, you could switch the money from your old pension into your new scheme. If your previous scheme was a stakeholder pension there will be no penalty for transferring but if it was a personal pension you will need to check if there is any charge for moving your money first.

must know

Pension transfers

See the Financial Services Authority's (FSA) factsheet: 'FSA guide to the risks of salary-related occupational pension transfers' available via its website www.fsa.gov.uk/consumer or tel: 0845 606 1234.

Topping up a work-based pension

Even if you belong to a good work-based pension scheme now, past periods when you did not have a pension, or did not save enough, may mean that your pension savings could do with being topped up.

There are various ways in which you can boost your savings depending on the type of pension scheme you belong to:

1) Additional Voluntary Contributions (AVCs)

If you belong to an occupational pension scheme, you may be offered an AVC scheme so you can make extra savings to top up your pension. Even if your main pension is salary related, AVCs are usually investment-based money-purchase schemes, so the more you put in the more you will get out. Charges on these schemes are usually low but the investment choices may be limited. Now members of occupational schemes can save in their own stakeholder pensions or personal pensions instead.

2) Added years

Members of salary-related schemes, usually in the public sector, may be able to purchase extra years of service to enhance their pension benefits. These are an expensive option, but they are secure as they provide a specific amount of extra pension. If you can afford it, this may be the best way to top up your final-salary pension.

3) Stakeholder and personal pensions

Members of occupational schemes can now make savings in stakeholder pensions or personal pensions as well. Also, if you already belong to an employer-based stakeholder or personal pension, you can increase your savings at any time. Your employer may be prepared to pay in more if you do. Or you could take out another stakeholder pension or personal pension plan if you feel the investment choices offered by your employer's scheme are too limited.

Future developments

A new type of pension scheme will be introduced in 2012. Everybody in a job who is not already in a company pension scheme will be automatically enrolled in a new National Pension Savings Scheme (NPSS). They will have 4% deducted from their pay towards this pension. Employers will put in another 3% and a further 1% will come from the Government in tax relief, making a total contribution of 8%. The money will go into individual pension accounts but exactly how it will be invested or which companies will provide the schemes still has to be sorted out. Employers that already offer pension schemes to which they contribute at least 3% will not have to offer the NPSS. It will not be compulsory for employees to join either type of scheme but if they do not they will sacrifice the employer and Government contributions to their pension. The self-employed and non-workers will also be able to opt into the NPSS.

If you are self-employed or work for a very small employer

When you are self-employed it is crucial that you have your own private pension. Not only will you not have any help from your employer with your pension, you will only get the basic state retirement pension. The self-employed do not pay into the State Second Pension. You will need to choose whether to take out a stakeholder pension or a personal pension.

If you are an employee of a small company with less than five employees you will also have to sort out your own private pension as your employer is not obliged to provide you with access to any kind of pension. You will also have to decide between a stakeholder pension and a personal pension.

Case study

Ajay, 36, is self-employed. He has not had a pension before and is not sure whether a stakeholder pension or a personal pension would be best for him. As he wants to keep costs to the minimum and doesn't want to be penalised for varying his savings if his income fluctuates he decides a stakeholder pension is the right option for him initially. This will not stop him taking out an additional personal pension in future.

Stakeholder pensions v. personal pensions

Stakeholder pensions and personal pensions are very similar. In both cases, you can normally invest your savings in a choice of investment funds (see chapter 4). The pension you get at retirement will largely depend on how much you have saved and how well your investments have performed.

The most appropriate first choice for most people is a stakeholder pension. If you are interested in what a personal pension might offer bear in mind that the basic terms and conditions on stakeholder pensions are laid down by Government whereas personal pension providers can set their own terms and conditions so you will need to be sure that you are getting a good deal. Here are some factors to take note of:

1) Your savings. With a stakeholder pension, the minimum amount you can save is £20. You can stop and restart your savings at any time without penalty. This can be particularly

must know

How much do you need?

You should already know how much extra you need to save if you did your sums in Chapter 2 – if not, turn back and do them now. For speed, use the Financial Services Authority's pension calculator – go to www.pension calculator.org.uk.

useful when you are self-employed and you have a fluctuating income. Personal pensions have become a lot more flexible in recent years but they may require higher savings, or a commitment to save regularly. Check that there are no penalties if you need to vary your savings.

2) Charges. Charges on stakeholder pensions are strictly limited. They must not exceed 1.5% per annum for the first ten years and then 1% thereafter, and any other charges must be optional. Some stakeholder pensions have lower charges. Personal pension providers can charge what they like. Competition has helped to bring charges down in recent years and some personal pensions can even work out cheaper than stakeholder plans. But it is important to check for initial charges or additional administration charges, which could reduce your savings. With stakeholder pensions you can move your savings to a new manager without penalty. This may not be the case with a personal pension.

3) Investment flexibility. Investment options may be limited under a stakeholder scheme. The only type of investment that stakeholder pension providers have to provide is a lifestyle fund where your contributions are normally invested in shares to start with. Then when you are within ten years of your expected retirement date the money is moved into safer investments, such as government bonds and cash. If you aren't interested in investment, this is probably all you need. But it is generally better to have a bit of choice so look out for stakeholder pensions that offer funds managed by outside investment managers, as this gives you some real scope. In a personal pension, you can have a much wider range of investment choices, especially if you choose a self-invested personal pension (SIPP – see box, right) but the charges may be higher. Don't take the personal pension route just for the extra investment choices unless you are going to make use of these investment options (for more on investment choices, see Chapter 4).

Which pension company?

Unless your employer has recommended a pension company, you will have to choose one for yourself. This often puts people off because they are worried about choosing the wrong company. Here are some ways you can narrow down the choice:

1. Stakeholder or personal pension?

Some companies offer both types of pension, others will offer one or the other. So the first step is to decide which you want. This will often boil down to what kind of investor you are. If you want something easy, cheap and straightforward a stakeholder pension is probably your best option. If you would like a greater choice of funds, a personal pension may be better. Neither decision is irreversible as you could switch from one type to the other at a future stage (although you need to check you won't be penalised for doing this in a personal pension).

2. Choice of funds

Whether you are choosing your own stakeholder or personal pension, it is better to have one that offers a range of funds to choose from, covering the main types of investments – UK and international shares, property, bonds and cash. Most pension companies will offer a selection of funds managed by their own

must know

What is a SIPP?

A SIPP is a self-invested personal pension. The actual pension wrapper is virtually the same as an ordinary personal pension. It is just that the pension company will let you decide for yourself where you want to invest your pension savings. You could, for example, choose which shares you wish to buy. This may sound like a good idea, but it is likely to be more expensive and more time-consuming that an ordinary pension plan and will not necessarily give you a better pension when you get to retirement. For more on SIPPs, see Chapter 4.

must know

Check the charges

One of the easiest ways to check out charges on stakeholder pensions and personal pensions go to the Financial Services Authority's (FSA) comparative tables at www.fsa.gov .uk/tables.

in-house investment teams. But it is even better to choose a policy that also offers access to funds run by external fund managers, normally specialist investment fund groups. This will mean you can achieve more diversification (see page 84 for more on the importance of this). No single investment company is good at managing all types of assets, although some make a better job of it than others.

3. Investment performance

The performance of the investments in your pension fund will have a major effect on how much retirement income it will generate. But predicting which pension companies are going to produce the best investment performance in the future is impossible. There are independent surveys of past performance of pension policies in magazines such as *Money Management* and *Investment, Life and Pensions Moneyfacts*. But bear in mind that past performance is no guide to the future. Pensions linked to specialist funds need to be treated with particular caution as they tend to be very volatile. Because of the unpredictability of future investment results it is a good idea not to put all your eggs in one basket – it is better to invest in a variety of funds managed by not just by your pension provider but by outside managers as well.

4. Charges

Performance may not be predictable, but charges are certain. It is important to make sure you do not pay over the odds for your pension. The advantage of stakeholder pensions is that charges are capped so they don't differ much from company to company.

With personal pensions there can be greater variations in charges so you will need to make more detailed comparisons between companies. Some people argue it is worth paying more if you are going to get better investment funds. But superior returns are never guaranteed. Personal pensions are not always more expensive than stakeholder pensions, though – investment trust personal pensions, for example, can be cheaper in the long run.

Key features

Before taking out a pension always look carefully at the 'Key Features' document that an adviser must provide. It explains four important points:

1) Product particulars. This will give information about the pension plan, outlining its aims, the risks and details of what you are committing yourself to.

2) The cost. You will be shown how much money will be taken out of your pension in charges. All companies must show the charges in actual monetary terms and explain how much they will reduce the investment growth on your savings.

3) Transfer values. A table is included that will allow you to see how much you have saved in each of the first five years compared with what the transfer value of the pension might be if you wanted to move your money to another pension company.

4) The cost of advice. This will reveal how much commission your adviser will receive so you can see how much you are paying for his or her advice (see page 79).

(see page 79).

must know

Unbiased advice

For impartial information on stakeholder pensions, go to the Pension Advisory Service's dedicated website www.stakeholderhelp line.org.uk or tel: 0845 601 2923. For other useful links go to www.stakeholder pensions.gov.uk. For a list of stakeholder pension providers go to www.stakeholder savings.gov.uk. See also the Financial Services Authority's (FSA) factsheet: 'Stakeholder pensions and decision trees' available through the website www.fsa .gov.uk/consumer or tel: 0845 606 1234.

Taking the plunge

Once you have decided on a stakeholder pension or personal pension, make sure it is one that gives you at least a 14-day cooling off period so you have time to change your mind after you have handed over your first savings. You will then be sent a 'Key Features' document. Make sure you read it through thoroughly and that it is what you expected. If not, ask further questions about anything you don't understand and if you are still not satisfied ask for your money back.

If you are not working

Career breaks created big problems for people in the past because they were not allowed to continue to save money in a pension so their retirement income suffered. But since the tax rules changed on the introduction of stakeholder pensions in 2001, it has been possible to make contributions – or for other people to make contributions on your behalf – to a stakeholder or personal pension even when you are not working.

You will still get basic-rate tax relief on your pension contributions even though you are not actually paying tax! The contributions you can make are limited but are probably enough for most people when they are not working. You can make net savings of up to £2,808 into your pension and the taxman will top it up with basic rate tax relief, increasing the amount invested to £3,600. Women who stay at home to care for younger children or elderly relatives should encourage their partners to help them top up their pension during this period.

If you move abroad

If your company sends you abroad and you are a member of the pension scheme, the company may allow you to remain a member and continue your contributions while you are away. If you already have a stakeholder or personal pension you can continue contributing and getting tax relief on up to £2,808 (made up to £3,600 with basic rate tax relief) for up to five years after you leave the UK. After five years, contributions can continue but no tax relief will be given.

You cannot start a new pension after you have left the UK and are no longer resident here. It is well worth considering contributing to a pension while you are away if you are planning to return to the UK in the future.

What to do when you have accumulated a number of pensions

These days, few people stay with the same employer throughout their working life unless they work in the public sector. This means you will often accumulate a number of different pension pots over the years, some in company schemes and some in individual policies.

This can make it difficult to keep track of exactly how much pension provision you have and to check whether your pension investments are performing as they well as they should be. This can be an argument for 'consolidation' – switching all your pension benefits into one plan such as a Self Invested Personal Pension (SIPP – see pp. 93-7), so you have a better overview and more control over your investments. But it is very important to consider any benefits you may be giving up if you move money out of an ex-employer's scheme, any transfer penalties you will incur if you transfer from an old-style personal pension and any guarantees you might lose. There can also be an argument for having your pension eggs in a number of different companies' baskets in order to spread your risk. Professional advice should always be sought if you are considering consolidation.

Finding a financial adviser

If you have found this chapter heavy-going and still feel confused about your pension options, it is worth considering seeking the help of a financial adviser. You may prefer the idea of going it alone, but bear in mind that if you choose the wrong pension plan, you will only have yourself to blame. If you have used a financial adviser who has sold you something unsuitable, you could qualify for compensation from the Financial Ombudsman Service. So using a financial adviser will give you more protection.

But you might feel apprehensive about this. How will you know how good the adviser is? Whether you can trust him or her? What the advice will cost? And how will you find a suitable adviser in the first place?

The good thing nowadays is that all advisers must be qualified and they are also obliged to keep up with relevant financial developments throughout their career; some take advanced qualifications. If you want someone who is more qualified look out for the initials AFPC (Advanced Financial Planning Certificate) or CFP (Certified Financial Planner) after their name. Advisers must also vetted by the City watchdog, the Financial Services Authority (FSA). Always check that any adviser you approach is authorised by the FSA, and to find out call the FSA Consumer Helpline on 0845 606 1234, or visit the FSA Consumer website www.fsa.gov.uk/consumer and follow the link to the Firm Check Service.

As to how much you will have to pay, you will normally get an initial interview with an adviser free of charge (but obviously check beforehand). At this interview you can ask about further costs. Before you put any money into a pension, your adviser will have to give you a 'Key Features' document anyway, which will include the cost of the advice.

There are three different types of adviser and this will affect the advice they can give you:

1) **Tied advisers**. These advisers work for one company so they can only advise on that company's pension products. Advisers working for most banks and building societies fall into this category.

2) **Multi-tied advisers**. These advisers can recommend the pensions of a number of companies, but the companies do not necessarily have to be the best on the market.

3) **Independent advisers**. These advisers deal with the whole pensions market and can advise you which company's pension is best for you. They may also be able to advise you about your employer's pension scheme. They must give you a choice of paying for their advice on a fee or commission basis.

The best option is to go to an independent adviser. If you are prepared to pay a fee, you are likely to get more holistic advice as the adviser won't have any need to sell you a product to pay for his or her time. Paying a fee may seem an expensive option compared to having the commission deducted from the pension you take out but it can work out cheaper in the long run.

There are various organisations that can help you find independent financial advisers in your area (see page 96). Get some names and visit two or three. This is time well spent as it is important that you feel comfortable with your adviser. Discuss what you want from your pension and choose an adviser who explains things clearly and doesn't make you feel dumb for asking questions.

want to know more?

• To compare the performance of different personal pension funds, read *Money Management* magazine, available from your newsagent or tel: 020 8606 7545.
• The FSA gives comparisons between stakeholder pension charges at www.fsa .gov/tables.
• See chapter 4 for a rundown of the different investments you can choose to put in your pension fund.
• For a list of organisations that can help you to choose a financial advisor, see page 96.

weblinks

• www.stakeholder pensions.gov.uk
• www.pension calculator.org.uk
• www.thepensions regulator.gov.uk
• www.opas.org.uk

4 Investing your pension

Consumers now have far more choice about
the way in which their pensions are invested,
whether in cash, bonds, property or equities.
The way you decide to allocate your assets
between different types of investment could
substantially alter the mount of money you
have to live on in retirement, so it's well worth
investigating the options.

Investing your pension

Remember that your pension is just a method of saving for retirement in a way that helps you pay less tax. With most types of pension you will be given a choice of where you want your savings invested. So how can you decide on the best investment? Are there any shortcuts?

Basic lifestyle funds

If you don't want to be bothered with investment issues, the simplest approach is to choose a 'lifestyle' investment fund. You will find these funds in all stakeholder pension plans and many company money-purchase pension plans too. The idea is that you can put your money into this type of fund and forget about it until you get to retirement.

How do they work? First of all your savings are invested in the stockmarket, usually in a tracker fund. A tracker fund follows the general movements in the stockmarket by buying roughly the same shares that are in FTSE All Share Index or the FTSE 100 Index – the main yardsticks of stockmarket progress. The reason for this is that over long periods of time shares have historically produced better returns than other types of investments.

When you are around ten years from your expected retirement date your savings will then be gradually switched into safer investment funds where your money will be held in cash or bonds. Bonds are loans to the government and companies. They pay a fixed rate of interest and are generally seen as more secure than shares. By the time you get to retirement all your pension saving will be in these safer funds and you won't have to worry about any last-minute fall in the stockmarket.

If you want to take more control over how your pension savings are invested, you will need to put some time and effort into it. You will need to learn about different types of investments and investment funds and what kind of returns they can offer as well as how much risk they involve. You will also have to find out how you can combine investments in your pension to get the best possible results at retirement. But the extra work could pay off.

Here are some questions you will need to think about before deciding on suitable pension investments:

1) How many years is it before you expect to retire?

2) If you already have a pension – where is it invested?

3) Which types of investments perform best over the long term?

4) How can you ensure the overall value of your pension savings doesn't fluctuate too much?

5) How can you find the best investment managers for your pension?

6) Do you want to actively manage your pension investments?

First principles

All types of investment involve some risk. Share prices rise and fall, but even with cash your returns will be affected if interest rates go down. Also, if the interest rate you get is not high enough there is the danger that rising prices (in other words, inflation), will mean the buying-power of your savings will go down over time.

Property is not immune from ups and downs either. In recent years people have come to regard buying residential property as the best investment there is, but they tend to overlook past price fluctuations. For example, in the first half of the 1990s there were five years in which average house prices either fell or did not move at all. This meant that people who bought properties in 1990 had to wait an average of seven years before they broke even again.

The best way to avoid taking too much risk with your pension is to spread your savings between different types of invest-ments. There are four main types of investments: shares, property, cash and bonds (which are loans to the Government, also known as gilts, or to companies).

Splitting your pension savings between different types of investments is a good idea because they don't all tend to move in the same direction at once. The chart opposite illustrates this point. It shows that when shares, as measured by the FTSE All Share Index, were falling in value between 2000 and 2003, government bonds i.e. gilts (Merrill Lynch UK), and property (Halifax) were rising while cash savings (Moneyfacts) crept up slowly but steadily. But the strong rise in share prices over the last twenty years shows they shouldn't be ignored despite their volatility. It's the old story – don't put all your eggs in one basket.

In the next sections are the types of funds you might want to mix and match in your pension and suggestions about exactly how you combine them to best effect.

Your main investment options

Pension companies normally offer a variety of investment funds, including the following.

How different types of investments have performed over the last 20 years

▬▬▬ FTSE All Share TR (IN)	▬▬▬ Merrill Lynch UK Gilt TR (IN)
▬▬▬ Halifax Property Seasonally Adjusted (IN)	▬▬▬ Moneyfacts Average Instant Access £25000 (IN)

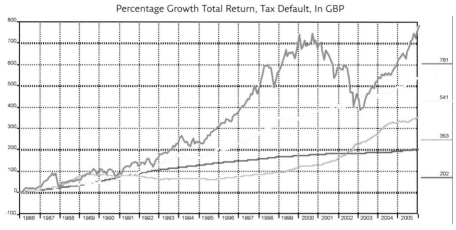

Percentage Growth Total Return, Tax Default, In GBP

20 Years From 31/12/1985 to 30/12/2005

Source: Lipper Hindsight

UK equities

Equities is another word for shares. UK equity funds normally invest in the shares of companies quoted on the London Stock Exchange. The investment managers running the funds spend their time trying to find attractively priced shares in companies they believe will generate increasing profits. Rising profits generally lead to rising share prices. They may look for companies that they believe have good prospects for recovery or those that may be subject to takeovers (which generally create a substantial increase in value for the shareholder). There is always a risk that a company could fail and its shares become worthless, but an investment fund will normally hold a large number of company shares, typically between 50 and 200, so that if one holding goes wrong it will not have a major impact on your overall investment.

A mainstream UK equity fund will normally invest in companies of different sizes ranging from leading household company names such as BP, Marks & Spencer, Sainsbury or HSBC down to smaller businesses that you haven't heard of but which could grow into large enterprises. Some UK equity funds are more specialist, focusing on larger or smaller companies only, or certain types of shares. Often the best approach is to invest in a mixture of different types of funds.

UK trackers

The difference between ordinary UK equity funds and UK tracker funds is that the managers of tracker funds do not try and buy and sell shares they think are doing well or badly. As already mentioned, tracker funds simply aim to follow a stockmarket index, such as the FTSE 100 Index, which charts the share price movements of the UK's largest 100 companies, or the FTSE All Share Index, which measures the progress of a cross-section of UK companies of different sizes.

The argument in favour of trackers is that many funds that are actively managed do not actually produce better returns than the stockmarket indices over the long term and some achieve significantly worse results.

If you invest in actively managed funds you need to monitor them regularly to check how well they are doing. With tracker funds this is unnecessary, as they will always perform in line with the index. Another advantage is that they often have significantly lower annual management charges than actively managed funds.

Managed

Managed funds have been a popular investment choice over the years for many pension savers. These funds usually hold a combination of shares, property, bonds and cash to provide a balanced investment portfolio. Investment managers may vary the mix of these investments to take advantage of changing investment conditions.

Nowadays, pension companies tend to offer a wider variety of managed funds for investors to choose from such as 'cautious managed', 'balanced managed' and 'active managed'. These have different mixes of investments and involve differing degrees of risk. Cautious managed, for example, is typically up to 60% invested in shares with the remainder in bonds, whereas active managed funds have a higher proportion invested in shares.

With profits

The most traditional type of pension fund is the 'with profits' fund. Like managed funds, with profits funds invest in a wide range of investments, including shares, property, bonds and cash. The main difference between with profits and other types of funds is in the way the investment returns are passed on to investors.

With most investment funds the returns on your savings reflect what is happening to the investments in the fund. Returns on with profits funds, on the other hand, are paid out in annual and final bonuses. The aim of the bonus system is to 'smooth' the fluctuations in the investment markets.

In recent years, with profits funds have become less popular after many companies had to cut back

must know

Choosing a fund manager

Don't go by one year's results alone. Look for a fund that has had the same manager and has performed well over a number of years. Websites www.trust net .co.uk or www.reuters.co.uk compare the performance of different funds. Every year, the best fund managers get awards from www.city wire.co.uk, while the worst funds are put in the doghouse by www.bestinvest.co.uk.

their bonuses significantly as a result of falling interest rates and poor stockmarket conditions between 2000 and 2003. Some of the stronger with profits companies with large reserves managed to maintain their bonuses at a higher level. But many investors nowadays are less keen on with profits funds because of the lack of transparency and the discretion retained by the company's actuaries who set the bonus rates.

Case study

Sally, 32, didn't really pay much attention to where her savings were going to be invested when she first started her stakeholder pension plan two years ago. She now realises she has ended up in the 'default' lifestyle fund, and her money is currently being invested in a UK tracker. She is okay with this but wants to increase her savings and spread her money around a bit. She decides to ask for her new contributions to go into a global equity fund.

Global equity

Investing in overseas stockmarkets through global equity funds is another way of spreading your investment risk. Stockmarkets in other parts of the world do not always move in tandem with the UK or US markets due to different economic conditions in those countries. So having part of your investments in these markets gives you greater diversification.

A global equity fund will invest in all the main international markets and some of the smaller ones including the emerging economies of the Far East and Eastern Europe. It may also include some exposure to the United Kingdom so it could provide a useful core holding to which you could add more specialist funds.

Your pension may also offer a range of funds investing in individual countries or regions, such as the US, Europe, Japan and the Far East. Some focus on emerging markets, such as China or India, which are often hailed as the most important economies of the future. However, they are much more volatile than Western stockmarkets and there are still political risks involved so don't go overboard. Another risk to be aware of when investing in overseas funds is that currency movements can affect your investment returns. If the yen collapses in value against the pound, your Japanese pension fund will be worth a lot less.

Ethical

A growing number of investors are reluctant to invest in funds that hold shares in companies involved in some sort of manufacture or trade of which they disapprove, such as armaments or pornography, or in those that do business with repressive regimes. Companies whose activities involve animal testing or factory farming, or have a negative effect on the environment, may also be off-limits for some investors.

A growing number of ethical investment funds are now offered that avoid investment in such companies and favour those that have positive policies towards their employees and the community. There remains an on-going debate about whether the returns on ethical funds can ever be as good as other funds. But, having said that, some ethical funds have performed very well.

Property

Property funds invest in commercial property, normally in a mixture of shops, office space and industrial buildings. They change the proportions in each type of property as economic conditions change. Sometimes they also invest in the shares of property companies as well as in bricks and mortar. Some funds concentrate on UK property, while others invest worldwide.

The main return on property funds comes from the rental income received from tenants although in recent years there has also been a significant rise in property prices as a result of an increase in investment in this area by large institutional investors. The Government has announced the launch of a new kind of property fund in 2007. These are called Real Estate Investment Trusts, or Reits for short. They are also expected to invest in commercial property at least initially. Reits will be more tax efficient than existing property funds when held inside a pension.

Property funds are regarded as less risky than equity funds because they invest in bricks and mortar. But these funds can still go down as well as rise in value.

Bonds

Bonds, also known as fixed interest securities, are issued by Governments and companies that want to borrow money from investors. They normally run for a fixed term and pay a fixed rate of interest, and at the end of the period the loan will be repaid to investors. During the term bonds can be traded on the stockmarket and their prices will fluctuate though not normally to the same extent as shares.

Returns on bonds reflect general interest rate expectations and as a result changes in the outlook for interest rates can affect the price of the bonds. The creditworthiness of the organisation that has issued them is another factor affecting bond prices. Government bonds are regarded as the most secure.

With corporate bonds there is a risk that the company may go bust and not be able to pay its

must know

Ethical pensions

If you are interested in finding out more about ethical investment or finding an independent financial adviser who can recommend an ethical pension, go to www.eiris.org.uk or tel: 020 7840 5700.

debts. But with financially strong companies this risk is very low – their bonds are described as 'investment grade'. Weaker companies have to pay higher interest rates to reward investors for taking more risk. Some bond funds invest purely in Government bonds, while others invest in investment grade or lower quality corporate bonds or a mixture of different types.

Bond funds are often recommended in the run-up to retirement because they are regarded as relatively secure and they tend to mirror movements in annuity rates since annuities are normally invested in bonds.

Deposit/cash

These are funds much like bank or building society savings accounts, attracting tax-free interest. While they provide a secure parking spot for your money, especially when investment conditions are uncertain, it is not a good idea to leave pension savings in cash for the longer term as the buying power of your savings is likely to be eroded by inflation. Other investments such as shares and property have proved better at beating inflation over the long term.

Getting the right combination

How you should divide your pension between different types of investment funds is described as 'asset allocation' – but it is not an exact science. It depends on how much risk you are prepared to take. This is often linked to your time horizon. The more time you have on your side, the longer you will have to ride out stockmarket ups and downs so the more risk you can afford to take. One old rule of thumb is that the proportion of savings you invest

must know

Types of bonds

The term bond is much over-used. Investment experts use it to describe fixed-interest investments issued by governments and companies. Banks and building societies use it to describe savings products that pay fixed rates of interest for a fixed period (usually one to five years). Insurance companies use it to describe a range of lump sum life insurance plans, such as guaranteed growth or income bonds, which pay fixed returns, and investment bonds, where returns depend on investment performance.

in low-risk assets such as bonds and cash should reflect your age. The remainder should go into riskier assets such as shares. So at age 30, for example, you should have only 30% in bonds and 70% in shares, at 50 you should have 50:50 and at age 70 you would have 70% in bonds and just 30% in equities.

You may ask why you should take risks at all? The answer is that historically shares and property have produced the best returns over longer periods so if you ignore them completely you will be depriving yourself of potential gains. This is why it is important to have a balance.

Which funds?

It is not only the type of funds but also the skills of the managers who run them that will affect the overall investment perform-ance of your pension. Nowadays many pension companies offer not just their own funds but also a selection of funds run by specialist investment managers. To check the track records of various funds look in publications such as *Money Management* (available on newsstands or tel: 020 8696 7545) or at web-based performance tables such as Trustnet (www.trustnet .com), or Morningstar at (www.morningstar.co.uk). Citywire also ranks investment managers according to the performance they have achieved – see www.citywire.co.uk.

The multi-manager approach

Most investment funds have a single investment manager deciding the best shares, bonds or properties to buy. But a single manager won't always be right and his or her style may be better suited to some investment conditions rather than to others. This is why it is a good idea to spread your pension savings between several managers as well as several different types of investment.

One increasingly popular way of doing this is through 'multi-manager' funds. These funds spread your money between a number of the funds that the manager believes are the best in

Planning your pension investments: suggested asset allocations

10 years or more to retirement	Asset allocation			
The emphasis should be on equities with a	UK Equities	30%	to	40%
wide geographical spread as all historical	Overseas Equities	35%	to	50%
analysis points to these providing the highest	Property	5%	to	10%
returns over the longest periods. You can	Bonds	5%	to	10%
afford to tolerate the higher volatility of equities	Other (inc. cash)	5%	to	10%
in the knowledge that you have plenty of time				
for market cycles to even out.				
5-9 years to retirement	Asset allocation			
Most of the portfolio should continue to be held	UK Equities	25%	to	35%
in equity funds, but the period until retirement	Overseas Equities	20%	to	30%
is in sight, so an increasing exposure to less	Property	10%	to	20%
volatile investments such as property and bond	Bonds	15%	to	25%
funds is desirable.	Other (inc. cash)	5%	to	15%
Less than 5 years to retirement	Asset allocation			
At this stage the protection of capital is	UK Equities	25%	to	35%
paramount, not just against sharp fluctuations in	Overseas Equities	15%	to	25%
equity markets but also falls in annuity rates.	Property	10%	to	20%
Consequently, an increasing emphasis on bond	Bonds	25%	to	35%
and property funds is the most appropriate	Other (inc. cash)	0%	to	10%
strategy during this time.				

Source: Bestinvest

a particular sector. Then if one of these managers starts to underperform or moves to another company, the manager of the multi-manager fund will decide whether to keep the fund or move to a new one.

The main drawback of these funds is that you pay two sets of management charges, one to the multi-manager and one to the underlying fund managers. This often amounts to over 2% per annum. However, it will mean your pension savings won't end up languishing in the worst performing fund because you haven't got round to checking it.

Taking control through SIPPs

If you want as much freedom as possible in where you invest your pension savings you could consider a Self Invested

Personal Pension (SIPP). This type of pension will enable you to invest directly in shares and choose from any investment fund, as well as from a range of other investments.

SIPPs have been available since the early 1990s but until quite recently you had to have a large pension fund of £100,000 or more for them to be cost effective. Nowadays growing competition among pension providers has brought SIPP costs down significantly and made them a potential choice for savers with say £5,000 or £10,000 to invest. However, they are still more expensive than ordinary stakeholder pensions or personal pensions and it is not worth paying the extra unless you are really going to make use of the investment flexibility they offer.

A SIPP can invest in commercial property so it may be attractive, for example, if you are self-employed or run a business and are interested in buying your own premises. A SIPP may also appeal if you have several pensions that you have accumulated with different providers or former employers over the years and you want to consolidate them in one place but still have plenty of variety in your investments.

These are the main investments that can be held in SIPPs:
• Quoted shares (shares in public companies listed on the stockmarket)
• Bonds (IOUs from governments or companies that have borrowed money from investors)
• Unit trusts
• Open-ended investment companies (different kinds of investment funds)
• Investment trusts
• Traded endowment policies (second-hand endowments which investors buy from the original owners)
• Futures and options (contracts that allow you to buy or sell shares at a fixed price some time in the future, also called derivatives)

- Insurance company funds
- Structured products (investments that can offer capital protection and pre-defined returns, usually linked to a stockmarket index)
- Hedge funds (high-risk funds that aim to take advantage of mispriced investments, sometimes using derivatives and borrowing)
- Commercial property and land
- Cash accounts

It is also possible to borrow up to 50% of the net value of the investments held within a SIPP to purchase other investments. This facility is particularly useful if you want to buy commercial property, for example premises for your business.

Case study

Rodney, 52, has been a member of an occupational money purchase pension scheme and a group personal pension scheme in the past and has left these pensions behind when he moved to new employers. He is now contributing to his current employer's money-purchase scheme but would like to save more. He would also like greater control over his pension investments so he has decided to transfer his old scheme benefits into a SIPP and put his extra savings in there too. He isn't interested in exotic investments and so has decided to choose a basic SIPP which allows him to invest in a wide range of investment funds and UK shares.

Choosing a SIPP

The first step in deciding which SIPP is best for you is to consider where you are likely to want to invest. Are you mainly interested in being able to access a wide choice of investment funds, stocks and shares and deposit accounts? Or do you want to be able to invest in commercial property and futures and options?

Some SIPPs offer more investment choices than others, but there is no point in signing up for a plan with lots of fancy bells and whistles that you are not going to use because you will generally have to pay more.

Here are some of the charges you may be asked to pay for a SIPP:

1) **A one-off set-up charge:** these can range from zero if you are choosing a basic SIPP that allows you to invest in the funds and shares of your choice, to over £700 if you want to have access to more wide-ranging investments.

2) **Transfer in fees:** if you want to switch benefits from another plan into your SIPP, there is likely to be a fee, typically £40.

3) **An annual administration fee:** this charge can also range from zero to over £600. Check exactly what it covers. With some plans it will cover all the basic administrative functions such as dealing with the taxman; others will charge additional fees for certain services. An annual valuation may be included, for example, but more frequent valuations may cost more.

4) **Transaction fees:** a charge may be levied for carrying out investment instructions. These are typically between £20 and £30. But some providers allow all or a certain number of transactions each year free of charge. If you want to buy property, there will also be legal and other fees to pay (survey, stamp duty and so forth).

5) Transfer-out fees: if your SIPP provider is not up to scratch you may want to move your money elsewhere so check the costs involved. A modest charge may be reasonable but you don't want to feel trapped.

Getting advice

While you may be attracted by the idea of controlling your own investments in a SIPP, in practice many people end up using the services of a professional, such as an independent financial adviser, investment manager or stockbroker, to advise them on their investment strategy. This will, of course, add a further layer of cost.

If you are going to ask an advisory firm to manage your investments find out about the investment returns they have achieved for clients in the past. Many advisers run model portfolios so they should be able to give you an idea of how these have performed. Ask to be put in touch with two or three existing clients to find out what their experience has been. This is perfectly acceptable practice. If you were hiring an au pair or a builder, you would check out their references first, so why not do the same with financial advisors?

want to know more?

• If you start read the money pages of your weekend newspaper, you will find tables comparing annuity rates, mortgage rates and savings account interest rates, as well as articles which often give useful advice on pensions, funds and other types of investment.
• You'll find information on specific companies at www.companyrefs.com. This is useful if you're thinking in investing in shares.
• See opposite for organisations that will help you to find a financial advisor.

weblinks

• www.eiris.org.uk (for advice on ethical pensions)
• www.trustnet.co.uk or www.reuters.co.uk (for comparing fund performance)

5 Approaching retirement

Around three to six months before you retire, there are a number of decisions to make, of which the most important is generally whether or not to buy an annuity. If you need one, should you opt for a level, escalating, index-linked or investment-linked policy? Should you have more than one, perhaps? What are the options if you decide against an annuity, and how can you make the best use of your retirement lump sum?

Approaching retirement

Even if retirement is just around the corner, you cannot afford to relax just yet. Unless you are getting a fixed income from a salary-related pension scheme, you need to think about where you can get the best pension from your pension savings.

must know

Claiming your state pension

If you have not heard from the Dept of Work and Pensions about three months before you are due to start drawing your state pension, contact the DWP on 0845 300 1084, or see the website www.thepensionservice.gov.uk. You can get free pension guides by calling 0845 731 3233.

The basics

It may come as a bit of a surprise to discover that the pension company you have saved with is not necessarily the one from which you should take your regular pension when you retire. It might be – but only if you have checked first that it is offering the best deal.

The reason for this is that at retirement your pension savings will normally have to be transferred into an annuity to give you a regular pension. An annuity is an insurance product in which you invest your pension fund that pays a guaranteed income for the rest of your life. Lots of insurance companies provide these annuities but some pay out much higher incomes than others.

So don't, whatever you do, just take the annuity offered by the pension company you have saved with – or from your employer if you have a job-related pension – without finding out if you could do better. You have the right to switch your pension savings elsewhere under what is known as the 'open market option'. This could boost your pension significantly for the rest of your life. It is not difficult or expensive to do, but you have to make the right decision, because once you have started drawing a pension you won't normally be able to withdraw your money and move it to a different annuity.

Here's a quick step-by-step guide to what you should do if you want to keep things as simple as possible (or see the decision tree on pp. 118-19):

1) Around three to six months before you are due to retire, ask your various pension providers for details of what pension you can expect and whether your pension includes a guaranteed annuity rate (some old-style pensions promised a minimum pension – for more on this, see below).

2) Decide whether you want to take part of your pension as a lump sum – most people do, since it is the most tax-efficient option.

3) Take the replies from your pension providers to an independent financial adviser. Make sure you go to a firm that specialises in annuities (see box, right, for help in finding one).

4) Discuss which type of annuity you are going to take with the adviser – most people go for a level annuity which pays a fixed income for the rest of their life but there are other options worth considering, particularly if your health isn't perfect (see page 107). If you have a spouse or partner without an adequate pension of their own, you will also need to consider an annuity that continues paying out an income after your death.

5) Let the adviser shop around for the best annuity on your behalf.

6) Now you can relax and start enjoying your retirement knowing you have bought the best possible pension with your savings.

A specialist adviser will do the job for you, but it is better if you have a rough idea of the annuity options so you can discuss the pros and cons knowledgeably.

must know

How to shop around for your annuity

Annuity rates can change rapidly and it is not always the same companies that offer the best deals so it is important to check the up-to-date rates. There are various comparison websites that show annuity rates (including the Financial Services Authority's comparative tables at www.fsa .gov.uk or Moneyfacts at www.moneyfacts.co.uk. These provide a useful guide but your circumstances may be different. It is usually better to get an independent financial adviser to shop around on your behalf. Specialist annuity advisers include www.annuity direct.co.uk, tel: 0500 506 575, www.william burrows.com, tel: 020 7421 4545, and www.annuitybureau .co.uk, tel: 0845 602 6263.

If you don't want to buy an annuity, there is another way of taking income from your pension. So if you would like to delve a bit deeper into what you can do with your pension savings when you reach retirement, read on. Here are some of the questions this chapter will look at in more detail:

1) Why is taking a lump sum from a pension normally a good idea?
2) How can annuities give you a good deal?
3) How is the pension you get from an annuity worked out?
4) What are the different types of annuities?
5) Why could taking some risk with your retirement savings pay off?
6) How can you leave your pension to others on your death?

First things first: when can you start taking your pension?

There are two different answers to this question:
• the retirement age specified by your pension scheme
• the minimum age for taking private pensions laid down by the Government.

In the first case, if you belong to a company pension scheme, there will usually be a 'normal retirement age' laid down by your employer at which you can take your pension. If you have taken out a personal pension you may have been asked for your 'selected retirement date' when you first started saving. If you want to retire early from these schemes you may be penalised. This is something you will need to check with your human resources department or pension provider if you are considering early retirement.

With a stakeholder pension, companies cannot impose penalties. Officially, the earliest age at which you can access a private pension at present is 50. Nowadays this also includes pensions used to contract out of SERPS, or the State Second Pension, where the minimum age for taking a pension used to be 60. In 2010 the minimum official age for taking a private pension will increase to 55.

You don't actually have to stop working in order to draw benefits from your pension, and these days you can take the tax-free lump sum without having to touch the rest. Some advisers have tried to encourage people to 'unlock' their pensions early in this way and use the money for other purposes. But it is not normally a good idea because it may mean you have less money available when you eventually stop working.

Case study

Desmond is nearly 65 and about to retire. His wife Kathie is 60. His pension fund will be worth £50,000 after he has taken tax-free cash of £16,650. His current pension provider has offered to convert his fund to an annual level pension of £2,440, guaranteed for five years (see page 109 for an explanation of this term). If he dies before Kathie, she will get two-thirds of this amount. To see if he can get a better deal, he goes to an annuity adviser who shops around and finds another company that offers an annuity, guaranteed for five years with a two-thirds widows' pension, that will pay him £2,855 a year making him over £400 a year better off throughout his retirement.

What happens at retirement?

If any of your pensions involve buying annuities – in other words, if you have a money-purchase company pension, AVCs, a stakeholder pension or a personal pension, don't leave it too near retirement to start planning your next move.

You will need to find out the size of your pension fund and start shopping around for the best annuity. This is known as using the 'open market option'. Don't expect your company or pension provider to encourage you to do this. It may not even

must know

Retiring soon?

For more general
information see the
Financial Services
Authority's factsheet:
'Retiring soon – what
you need to do about
your pensions', available
at www.fsa.gov
.uk/consumer or tel:
0845 505 1234.

be clear from the letters they send you that this
option is available. But it is your right and one you
should use if you want to make sure you are going
to get the best possible pension.

WARNING: Before shopping around, check
whether your pension offered a guaranteed annuity
rate. These arrangements, available on some old-
style personal pensions and retirement annuities,
were set up when interest rates were much higher
than they are today so you could be better off staying
with your current provider.

Should you take a tax-free lump sum?

The answer for most people is yes. Even if you do not
have anything specific you want to spend it on, taking
a lump sum is usually recommended for tax reasons.
This is because a lump sum is tax free, whereas if
you take extra pension it will be liable to income tax.

If you need extra income from your lump sum,
you can then invest it to produce a more tax-
efficient income. For example, one way of investing
your tax- free lump sum where it will provide tax-
free income is to put it into an Individual Savings
Account (ISA) linked to a bond fund. The maximum
amount you can place in an ISA is £7,000 each tax
year so, depending on the size of your lump sum,
you may have to spread your investment over
several years.

If you want a fixed income from your lump sum,
you could even buy a different type of annuity,
known as a 'purchased life annuity'. The advantage
of this type of annuity over a pension annuity is that
part of the income is treated as a return of your
capital and is tax free, so you would pay less tax.

However, the returns on these annuities are not regarded as very competitive at the moment. (See Chapter 8 for other ways of investing your lump sum.)

How much tax-free cash?

It is now possible to take at least 25% of your private pension fund as tax-free cash, providing the scheme rules allow it. This also applies to contracted-out personal pensions and additional voluntary contributions (AVCs) started after April 1987 where tax-free lump sums were previously not permitted.

If you have taken out AVCs in conjunction with a salary-related pension scheme, it may be preferable to take as much of your lump sum from your AVC fund as possible. This way you can maximise the pension you get from your salary-related scheme which will be increased in line with inflation (up to a limit of 5%). Buying this type of pension with your AVCs would be a lot more expensive. But whether this is possible will depend on your main pension scheme rules.

must know

Special rules for small pension funds

If your pension funds are modest, you may be able to take them all in cash. The limit on these 'trivial' pensions is £15,000 in the 2006-07 tax year or 1% of the lifetime pension allowance. You will only be able to take 25% of your pension fund tax free, though, and you will have to pay income tax on the rest. To take advantage of this concession, you must be aged between 60 and 75 and take all your pensions as cash within a one-year period.

Annuities - the good, the bad and the ugly

After taking a lump sum, most people will need to use the remainder of their pension fund to buy an annuity. Annuities have attracted a bad press in recent years but they have got some real advantages.

One of the major complaints about annuities is that the amount of pension they pay has gone down significantly. This is mainly due to falling interest rates. Annuities normally invest in bonds, such as Government bonds and high-quality corporate bonds (bonds issued by blue-chip, financially strong companies), and the returns they pay are determined by general interest rates. But they are not the only investments to have been hit by falling interest rates. Rates on savings accounts are now only around a third of what they were 25 years ago.

The other factor that has affected annuity rates is that we are all tending to live longer so companies have had to adjust annuity payments to spread them over longer periods.

But the important plus-point to remember about annuities is that they can guarantee you an income for life no matter how long you live and no matter what happens to the financial markets. You could not get that guarantee from any other type of investment.

If you really do not want to buy an annuity, there are ways of taking an income direct from your pension fund instead. But be warned – although this approach may sound good in theory, it is a risky option and is only likely to be a suitable choice for a minority of people with very large pension funds.

When you buy an annuity the amount of pension you will get will depend on a number of factors, some of which you can influence and some you cannot. Here are the main ones.

Things you can't change

1) Your age. Annuity rates increase with age. So the older you are when you start taking your pension, the more you will get per year. This is because insurance companies aim to spread the payments from your capital over the rest of your life. The older you are, the fewer years the money will need to stretch. However, don't assume you will get a better deal by waiting until you are older to buy an annuity. As time passes people are living longer and this trend has been gradually pushing annuity rates down. For this reason the rate you get now may actually be better than you would be able to get in five years' time even though you will be five years' older.

2) Your sex. Women get lower annuity rates and therefore lower pensions than men of the same age for the same amount of money because women are expected to live longer.

3) Your state of health. Insurance companies generally assume you are in good health when you buy an annuity and will offer you an income based on the average life expectancy for someone your age. If you are in poorer health, though, they reckon that you won't live so long. Fortunately, nowadays, there are companies that will take your health into account and if they think you will not live as long as average, they will give you a higher income per annum. Health problems which are likely to reduce your life expectancy include diabetes, severe asthma, cancer or heart problems. Subject to medical evidence about your condition, you may be able to get an income that is up to 30% higher than standard annuity rates. However, if you are in a very poor state of health it may be a better idea to consider taking an income direct from your pension fund – usually known as an 'income drawdown' (for more details on this see pp. 113-14) as this will mean that if you die prematurely any capital remaining in your pension fund (less 35% tax) can be passed on to your family or other beneficiaries.

4) Your lifestyle and occupation. If you are overweight, a regular smoker or do a manual job you may also be able to get a better annuity. If you have smoked at least ten cigarettes a day for the last ten years, you could be eligible for higher rates. And your income won't change even if you later give up smoking. At least one annuity provider also pays more if you are a manual worker from the West Midlands, Northern England, Scotland, Wales and Northern Ireland as statistically you have a lower life expectancy than the rest of the population.

Things you can influence that will affect your annuity rate

1) Who gets the pension? When you buy an annuity you will have a choice of buying one that pays an income to you only or to you and your partner. If you buy one that pays an income just to you – a so-called single life annuity – the income will normally stop when you die. But if you buy a joint life annuity it will continue paying out an income to your partner after you die. A joint life annuity is therefore usually the best choice if you are married or have a long-term partner who does not have an adequate pension of their own. There will be a price to pay for this – it means you will get less income to start with, but the total amount of income paid out could potentially be much higher in the long run if your partner outlives you by several years.

The reduction in your income will partly depend on how much income you want your annuity to pay out after your death – it can remain the same but this is the most expensive option. It will be cheaper for you if payments reduce by, say, a third or a half after your death providing this will give your partner enough to live on. Bear in mind that if your partner dies before you, you won't be able to claim a higher income again. It's a gamble!

But if your pension includes a guaranteed annuity rate that only applies to the purchase of a single life annuity it may be better to go for that – even if you have a partner. Guaranteed rates tend to be much higher than current annuity rates, so you could use some of the extra income to, say, take out a life insurance policy which will pay money to your partner on your death instead.

must know

Life expectancy

If you delay taking out an annuity till age 75, you may find the rates do not increase proportionately in your favour. Many insurance companies take the view that those who make it to 75 without major health problems are tough old birds who could end up getting their telegram from the Queen and costing them a fortune!

2) **Frequency of pension payments**. You can decide how often you want your pension paid out: monthly, quarterly, half yearly or yearly, either in advance or arrears. By waiting longer between payments, you can boost your pension – quarterly payments, for example, are likely to be around 1.5% to 2% higher than monthly ones. But most people prefer the convenience of monthly payments.

3) **How long your pension is going to be paid**. Normally annuity payments will stop when you die, unless you have taken out a joint life annuity. So if you die shortly after taking out the annuity, this means most of your money will disappear into the insurance company's coffers. One way to ensure your beneficiaries get some money in these circumstances is to choose an annuity that pays out for a guaranteed period, typically five or ten years, even if you die within that period. Opting for a five-year guarantee will not make much difference to your income, but a ten-year guarantee will cost more.

4) **What happens to your capital**. Since April 2006 it has also been possible to buy annuities – called 'value-protected annuities' – that will pay out to your family or other beneficiaries whatever capital is left in your annuity if you die before you are 75. So, for example, if you put your pension fund of, say, £50,000 into a value-protected annuity at age 65 and got an annual pension of £3,000 a year for five years before you died at age 70, you would have received a total of £15,000. This would leave a balance of £35,000 which could be paid back to your estate, less tax of 35%. You will have to pay for value protection by receiving a lower pension. If you don't die by 75, you will have lost quite a lot of pension for nothing.

must know

Life insurance – who needs it?

If your partner or children depend on your income, then you should take out life insurance to protect them if you should die before they attain independence.

> ## Don't leave it to your employer
> It is not just those who have taken out their own stakeholder pensions or personal pensions or AVCs that need to think about their retirement income options. If you belong to a job-based money-purchase pension scheme, your employer will normally arrange to buy an annuity on your behalf. But you may not get the best possible deal, especially if you are a smoker or have suffered a health problem. You may get a better income by asking if you can shop around yourself – with the help of an adviser.

must know

Annuity shopping

The difference between the best and worst annuity rates at any given time could mean your income is 10-15% more or less for the rest of your life. That's why it pays to shop around carefully.

Types of annuities

The amount of pension income you receive will also be influenced by the type of annuity you buy. There are four main types:

1) Level. As the name implies, the payments from these annuities remain fixed for the rest of your life. They will often give the highest pension of any type of annuity when you first retire. The amount of pension you get will largely depend on long-term interest rates at the time you retire. Your payments will not be affected if interest rates rise or fall in the future. The main drawback with this type of annuity is that your pension's purchasing power will not remain the same because of rising prices. Although inflation is currently only in the region of 2.5% a year, even at this rate after 10 years your income will be worth around 20% less and after 20 years it will have fallen by 40%. That's a big difference!

2) Escalating. With these annuities, your pension will increase at a fixed percentage each year, say 3%. This may sound attractive but the disadvantage is that your pension will start at a lower rate than it would with a level annuity and will take some years to catch up and several more years before the total pension you have received is more. If you outlive the standard life expectancy you will do better with an escalating annuity but you are taking a risk. It may be preferable to take a higher level pension and save any income you do not need to spend until later.

3) Index-linked. Pensions from these annuities will rise each year in line with the Retail Price Index, like the state pension. This gives you the peace of mind of knowing that your pension's purchasing power will be maintained, but your initial income will be lower than from a level annuity. Unlike escalating annuities, it is impossible to predict how long it will take for an index-linked pension to match a level pension. If you think inflation may surge ahead these annuities are worth considering, but most experts believe a major upturn in inflation nowadays is unlikely.

4) Investment-linked. The ideal pension annuity would be one that starts at a reasonable level and increases year by year so your income keeps up with inflation. The nearest thing to that is an investment-linked annuity, but with these there is also the risk that your pension could go down. Investment-linked annuities come in two forms – with profits and unit-linked. The pensions from these annuities will depend on the performance of the investments so if the stockmarket nosedives your pension could fall. On the other hand, if investment performance is

must know

Annuity factsheet

For more information on annuities see the Financial Services Authority's factsheet: 'FSA Guide to pensions 3 – annuities and income withdrawal', available at www.fsa.gov.uk/consumer or tel: 0845 505 1234.

good your pension will rise. BEWARE: An investment-linked annuity should not be your only source of pension.

Case study

Caroline, 59, is about to retire and knows she will be getting a decent-sized pension from her salary-related scheme. She has also made additional voluntary contributions (AVCs). She is going to take 25% of her AVC fund as tax-free cash (she wanted to take more but her main pension scheme rules dictate that part of the benefits from that scheme must be taken as cash). So she has to decide what type of annuity to buy with the remainder of her AVC fund. As she is not desperate for extra income to start with, she decides to buy a with profits annuity so there is a chance the pension she gets from her AVCs will increase in future.

Mix and match

Buying pension annuities does not have to be an all-or-nothing decision. If you need the maximum pension you can get as soon as you retire to supplement your state pension, you will have little choice but to go for a level annuity because you will also need security, but if you have some leeway it is worth considering buying a mixture of different types of annuities.

Buying different annuities is easy if you have several different pension plans, and personal pensions are often set up as a number of policies which makes it possible to split them between different annuities if you want to. You will still probably want a level annuity to provide most of your pension so you know you have enough income to pay the bills and get by on, but the remainder of your pension could come from an index-linked or investment-linked annuity.

What your pension fund might buy you

Pensions payable from different types of annuities, assuming a pension fund of £50,000. All figures assume payments made monthly in advance.

	Level annuity with 5 yr guarantee	RPI linked annuity*	With profits annuity with 3% bonus anticipated*
Single pension			
Man			
age 60	£3,035	£1,995	£2,994
age 65	£3,485	£2,425	£3,428
Woman			
age 60	£2,825	£1,740	£2,842
age 65	£3,165	£2,115	£3,171
Joint pension (including 100% widow's pension)			
Man 60, Woman 60	£2,460	£1,470	£2,546
Man 65, Woman 60	£2,545	£1,550	£2,627

*No guaranteed periods   Source: Investment, Life & Pensions Moneyfacts

The only problem with this approach is that you may be limited by the minimum investment required for each annuity. Some companies won't accept less than £10,000 and a few have even higher limits.

Alternatives to annuities

It is now possible to avoid buying an annuity when you retire under new rules which came into force on 6 April 2006. You can leave your pension pot invested and take an income directly from your investments instead, as you would from other savings. In theory, this choice is open to all. In practice, it is normally only worth considering if you have savings in a pension fund of at least £100,000. The rules governing how you can take income from your pension fund savings without buying an annuity varies according to your age.

If you are under 75

Below the age of 75 you can take what is officially known as an 'unsecured pension', from your pension pot. It is often called 'income drawdown'. Most pension companies offer this option nowadays. You can choose how much pension you want to take – within certain limits. The maximum is 120% of what you could have got if you used these savings to buy an ordinary level pension annuity. The minimum is nil – you might choose to take no income if you need your tax-free lump sum but don't need a regular pension, say, because you are still working.

The maximum income limit has to be reviewed every five years. If annuity rates go down as they have in recent years, due to improving life expectancies and declining interest rates, you may find the amount of pension you can take is reduced after such a review. The income you can take will also be affected by how well the investments in your pension pot have performed. If they go down in value your income may also need to be reduced. So you won't have the same certainty about your pension as you would with an ordinary level annuity.

When you reach 75

Until 6 April 2006, it was compulsory to buy an annuity with your pension fund by age 75 at the latest. Now you can take an 'alternatively secured pension' instead. This is similar to income drawdown but the amount of pension you can take is more limited. You can still choose to take no income at all but if you do want an income the maximum is 70% of the pension that you could get from an ordinary level annuity at age 75. So it may be lower than the income you had been drawing prior to age 75. The maximum income level must be reviewed every year, so it may also be affected by fluctuations in your

must know

Income drawdown

If you are considering taking income drawdown you must take independent financial advice. See also the Financial Services Authority's factsheets: 'Income Withdrawal –a retirement option for you?' and 'Income withdrawal – pension changes', available at www.fsa.gov.uk/consumer or tel: 0845 606 1234.

investments. The main reason for limiting the income in this way is to ensure your fund lasts for the rest of your life.

The pros and cons of not buying an annuity

You may be attracted by the idea of not buying an annuity with your pension savings but for most people annuities will still be the best choice. Here are the main factors you need to weigh up when deciding on your options.

The pros:

Death benefits: For many people the main attraction of not converting their pension savings into an annuity is that they can leave the capital to their family in their will. If you die before age 75, the balance of your fund can be paid out as a lump sum, less a tax charge of 35%. Alternatively, if you have a husband, wife or civil partner or children under age 23, they can continue to draw an unsecured pension or buy an annuity with the remaining fund.

If you die after age 75 while taking an alternatively secured pension, your pension fund must be used to provide dependants' pensions (if you have any). If there are no dependants on your death, the remaining funds may be reallocated to provide pension benefits for other people nominated by you who are members of the same pension scheme. But these funds will be subject to a tax charge of 35% and will be liable to Inheritance Tax as well.

Investment control. Not buying an annuity means your pension savings can remain invested in the stockmarket and other investments where they can

must know

Changing your mind

If you opt for income drawdown or an alternatively secured pension, you can convert to a lifetime annuity at any time.

must know

A halfway house

As an alternative to buying an annuity for life, you can now use part of your pension fund to buy a fixed-term annuity lasting up to five years. The rest of your pension fund can remain invested. After five years you can buy another short-term annuity. You can continue doing this until you reach age 75.

potentially increase in value. Some people decide to transfer their pensions to self-invested personal pensions (SIPP) so that they have greater control over how their savings are invested at this time.

The cons:

Time and money. If you leave your pension fund invested after retirement, you will have to go on paying annual investment management charges. You will also have to be prepared to monitor your investments regularly to make sure you are getting a reasonable level of returns or pay a professional adviser to do it for you, which will add to the cost.

Risk. Income drawdown is a high-risk approach. You will have to invest most of your pension fund in the stockmarket if you want to ensure that your investments have a good prospect of producing enough income and maintaining their value against inflation over the long term. But this means they will go up and down in value as share prices fluctuate. Will you still be able to sleep at night if there is a prolonged downturn in the stockmarket?

Income. Your first priority when you get to retirement should be your own income require-ments rather than what happens after your death. An unsecured or alternatively secured income is not guaranteed in the same way as the payments from an annuity are. If there are a few bad years of investment returns, your pension fund and the income you can take from it could fall in value.

Is delaying buying an annuity a good idea?
Some people think it is a good idea to delay buying an annuity with your pension because annuity rates

increase with age. But the improvements are not as good as they look. The problem is that the later you buy your annuity the less you benefit from the cross subsidies from others in your age group who die earlier than average. Other factors have worked against those who have delayed buying an annuity in recent years.

Poor stockmarket conditions have meant that the investment performance of most pension funds has not been good enough for older people to buy the same amount of pension as they would have done if they had bought an annuity as soon as they retired. Annuity rates have also been going down due to a combination of decreasing interest rates and increasing life expectancies. As a result, even if investment returns had been sufficient to preserve the same capital value of a pension fund, an older investor would now get a lower pension than he would had he bought his annuity at the first opportunity. This has meant that most people who have delayed buying annuities in recent years have ended up with a lower overall income.

want to know more?

- See over page for an annuity decision tree to help you make up your mind.
- See page 101 for a list of all the ways you can compare the annuity rates offered by different companies. For a quick roundup, look in the money pages of your weekend newspaper.
- When you reach the age of 60, make sure you are applying for all the benefits to which you are entitled such as subsidised rail travel (tel: 0845 748 4950), winter fuel payments (tel: 0845 915 1515) and any other local arrangements such as free bus travel (call your local council).

weblinks

- www.moneyfacts .co.uk (for annuity rate comparisons)
- www.thepension service.gov.uk (advice on how to claim your state pension)

Annuity decision tree

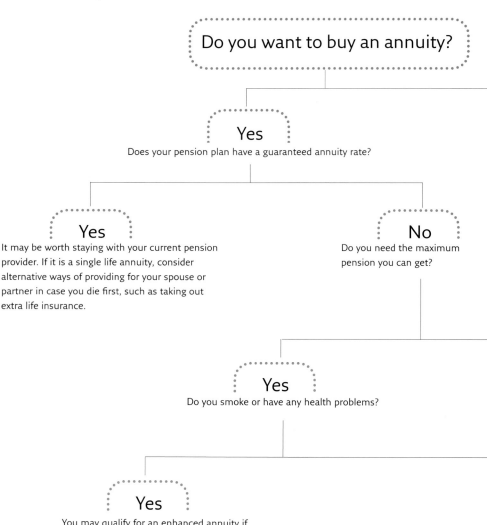

Do you want to buy an annuity?

Yes

Does your pension plan have a guaranteed annuity rate?

Yes

It may be worth staying with your current pension provider. If it is a single life annuity, consider alternative ways of providing for your spouse or partner in case you die first, such as taking out extra life insurance.

No

Do you need the maximum pension you can get?

Yes

Do you smoke or have any health problems?

Yes

You may qualify for an enhanced annuity if it is thought you have a reduced life expectancy.

No

Is your pension fund worth at least £100,000?

Yes

An income drawdown scheme is an option but you must take independent financial advice.

No

If you are worried about the insurance company getting your capital when you die, consider buying a 'value-protected' annuity.

No

Consider buying a combination of level and investment annuities. By putting part of your pension into an investment annuity you could get some income growth in the future providing you are prepared to take some risk

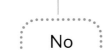

No

Shop around for the best level annuity using a specialist annuity adviser.

6 Pension planning for couples

Wouldn't you like to think that if you die before your partner, he or she will be able to continue drawing the pension you have taken such care to save? This probably won't be the case if you are not married or in a civil partnership, and it may not be cut and dried even if you are. If you get divorced, how can pension rights be split? And should you take out life insurance? Read on, for an explanation of pension planning for two.

Pension planning for couples

Pension planning is not something that many young couples are likely to discuss over a candlelit romantic dinner – but perhaps it should be. In a long-term relationship, pension savings can become a very important part of the family finances.

Do's and don'ts

Even though retirement may seem a long way off when you first begin your life together, there are still some basic 'do's' and 'don'ts' that you should bear in mind:

Do

• Do make sure you are both putting enough in your pensions – you will end up a lot better off in retirement than if only one partner bothers to save.

• Do agree beforehand that if one partner takes a career break, say to care for young children or an elderly parent, that the other will help top up the non-working partner's pension.

• Do find out basic details about your partner's pension so you know who to contact if he or she dies.

• Do remember you can get tax relief on your life insurance premiums if you buy a policy in conjunction with your pension.

• Do consider putting some money into your children's pensions if you want to help them save for the long term.

Don't

• Don't shy away from discussing pension planning with your partner. It's not as boring as it sounds – think about all the nice things you want to do when you retire.

• Don't overlook your partner's pension needs when you are buying an annuity at retirement.
• Don't rely on your partner's pension – it may not be enough and you may split up before retirement anyway.
• Don't underestimate the importance of your partner's pension if you divorce.
• Don't forget you will have no claim on your partner's pension if you split up unless you are married or in a civil partnership.

If you and your partner both plan your pensions seriously, particularly in your early years together, you have a good chance of being able to build up a significant pension income between you. When you retire you will then be able to afford to do all the things together that you did not have time to do when you were both busy working.

The difference between men and women

There should be no real difference between men and women when it comes to pensions. It is equally important for both sexes to save enough so they have an adequate retirement income. Indeed, for women, who can expect to live longer than men and therefore spend more years in retirement, it could be argued that it is even more important.

Unfortunately, however, women have tended to give pensions an even lower priority than men. In the past, married women often opted to pay a special lower rate Married Women's National Insurance contribution, which means that many who are now retired don't even qualify for a basic state pension in their own right.

did you know?

Women and state pensions

Currently only 50% of retired women receive a full basic state pension and women are nearly twice as likely to receive means-tested pension benefits as men.

Nowadays women of working age have to pay full National Insurance contributions if they are working and if they are at home looking after children or an elderly relative they can claim Home Responsibilities Protection (for details see Chapter 2, page 35), so are more likely to be building up full state pension rights. But they are less likely than men to be putting savings into a private pension. Some 46% of men are building up a private pension compared to only 38% of women, according to the Pensions Policy Institute.

Younger women, though, are becoming more aware of the importance of pensions. Interestingly, the only age group where more women than men are saving in a pension is among 18–29 year olds. Any savings you can make at this age are particularly important as there is a lot more time for your money to grow before you reach retirement than with savings you make later in life. For women who think they may want to take time off work for family reasons, saving as much as you can as early as you can is crucial.

This is easier said than done, of course, as many younger women and men face other demands on their income, such as repaying their student debts and saving the deposit for their first home. If you are faced with this situation, the first priority should be to pay off expensive debts such as credit card bills. After that, and once you have some cash in the bank or building society to pay for emergencies, try splitting your savings between a pension and your other savings goals.

Even women who do start saving in a pension when they are young tend to find it difficult if they have children. Research shows that once women have a family, they tend to prioritise their children when it comes to spending, rather than putting money into their pension. Men, on the other hand, continue to make pension savings even after they have a family.

One thing's for sure: women need to start giving their retirement a much higher priority.

How the sexes compare in the pension stakes

Proportion of working-age people with a private pension

Age	Women	Men
18-29	24%	23%
30-39	43%	57%
40-49	46%	62%
50-60/65	40%	43%
All	38%	46%

Source: Pensions Policy Institute 2005

What couples should do to improve their pension

Surveys show that many women still rely on their husbands or partners to provide a pension to support them in retirement. Not only does this assume that their husbands' pensions are adequate for both of them, but it also takes for granted that they will still be together when they reach retirement.

Both of these assumptions could prove flawed. Although men are more likely to have a pension than women, many men still don't save or don't save enough to provide their wives with the standard of living in retirement that they would like. What's more, with so many marriages ending in divorce nowadays, there is no guarantee that a woman will still be married by the time she reaches retirement age.

Women are better advised to make their own pension savings. If their relationship continues, their pension will contribute to a much more comfortable retirement for them both. If it doesn't, at least they will have their own pension scheme when they go their own ways.

Each partner in a relationship will benefit from encouraging the other to make their own pension savings whatever happens. If they remain together it means the whole family unit will enjoy a higher income. If the relationship breaks down they will also gain as they are likely to be able to retain more of their own pension after the divorce settlement or civil partnership breakup.

Case study

Judith, 33, stopped work last year to look after her newborn son Charlie. She expects to be at home for about five years and is worried about the gap in her pension planning. She had been a member of stake-holder pension scheme at work and would like to keep making some contributions. She and husband Mark have some savings in the building society and agree to invest some of this money in her pension where it will immediately be worth more when basic rate tax relief is added. They decide to invest the maximum of £2,808 this year which will be topped up to £3,600 by the taxman.

Fortunately, nowadays even if a woman stops working to look after children or works part-time for a modest wage, it is still possible for her to put savings into a stakeholder pension or personal pension, or for someone else to do it on her behalf. There are considerable tax advantages to doing this as tax relief will be given on these savings even to non tax payers. Everyone is allowed to save at least £3,600 in a pension and because you get basic rate tax relief on these contributions it means you only actually need to pay £2,808. The taxman will pay the additional £792 in tax relief to top up your savings to £3,600 at the request of your pension company.

It is not only before retirement that there may be tax advantages in spreading a family's pension savings between both partners. After retirement if only one partner has a pension, it means only one person's personal tax allowance can be set against the pension income. If both have a pension then both partners' personal allowances can be utilised. For example, a couple in their late sixties who received the state pension plus an annual private pension income of £15,000 in one partner's name, would have to pay tax in the region of £2,400 in the 2006–07 tax year, but if the private pension was split with one receiving £10,000 and the other £5,000, their annual tax bill would go down to around £1,500, saving them £900 in tax.

Keeping it in the family

Parents or grandparents who want to make long-term savings for children to help them in their adult lives can now consider putting money into a pension on their behalf.

Future generations are likely to find it even harder to save enough for their retirement than we do today so any early help from older family members will stand them in very good stead in years to come.

There is no minimum age at which a stakeholder or personal pension can be taken out for a child. It is a very tax-efficient way of saving for youngsters who, like adults, qualify for basic rate tax relief on pension contributions of up to £3,600. This means the saver only needs to pay in £2,808 and the taxman will pay the rest to the pension company. The only disadvantage for children is that they will not be able to get at the money until they reach the age of 55.

What happens to your pension if your relationship breaks down?

It will all depend first of all on the status of your relationship.

Not married? No civil partnership?

Many couples choose to live together rather than getting married or entering into a civil partnership. When young, many people do not see much advantage in an official union. But when it comes to pensions, if a relationship breaks down there is a big difference between living together and being married or in a civil partnership.

Contrary to popular belief there is no such thing as a common-law marriage. So if you split up you will have no claim on your partner's pension. If you don't get married or enter into a civil partnership, you must therefore be even more careful about making your own pension savings otherwise you could be left high and dry without any pension if your relationship breaks down.

Divorcing? Dissolving a civil partnership?

A couple's pension savings are often one of their most important investments, second only to the family home (or ahead of it in some cases). If they divorce or their civil partnership is dissolved, a court will have to take the value of their pension benefits into account when the financial settlement is being determined.

This was not always the case. In the past, a lack of knowledge about the value of pensions among women and their solicitors often led to them being overlooked in divorce settlements leaving many women in financial hardship when they reached retirement. Now there are three ways in which the value of pensions can be divided up when a couple divorce or dissolve a partnership:

• **Offsetting**. Here the value of pension savings a couple has is balanced against the other savings and property they own. If one partner has most of the pension savings, the other one might get the rest of

---

must know

Scottish law

In the past, courts in Scotland could declare you married even if you never went through an official ceremony but could prove that you lived together as 'man and wife'. The law has now changed but co-habiting couples in Scotland do have other rights. This may still not give you any claim over your partner's pension if you split up, but if your partner dies before retirement the pension provider will take your relationship into account.

the assets instead. So one may get the family home, for example, and the other get to keep his or her pension. The problem with this approach is that one partner may be left with no pension at all and may eventually be forced to sell the family home or release equity (see page 162) to fund their retirement. It can be a risky strategy as property values will not necessarily keep on rising, whereas pension fund investments tend to be more diversified and over the long term are likely to outperform the residential property market. So what may seem like an equal division of the couple's wealth at the time of a divorce may not be so fair in the long run.

• **Earmarking/Attachment Orders**. This divides one partner's pension up so the other gets a part of it at retirement. The way it is done is that a court orders the pension scheme to pay part of the future pension to the former husband, wife or civil partner. The order only comes into effect when the person whose pension it is actually starts drawing his or her pension. If that person dies beforehand, the order will lapse, although attachment orders can also be made against any lump-sum death benefits to which the ex-spouse might have been entitled. This type of earmarking may take place if the value of the pension is not particularly great at the time of the divorce but is expected to grow in the future. This way the former partner will benefit from this growth. However, there are disadvantages. There is no clean break in this situation and if the ex-spouse or partner remarries or enters another civil partnership, they will lose their right to any of the pension.

• **Sharing**. With pension sharing the pension benefits are divided up at the time of the divorce.

must know

Financial orders

To find out more about pensions and divorce if you live in England and Wales, get the guide *I Want to Apply for a Financial Order* (form D190) from your local county court or www.hmcourts -service.gov.uk.

This may be done in one of two ways – with an occupational pension scheme the ex-spouse or partner may become a member of scheme themselves with their own pension rights, or alternatively a lump sum may be paid into a separate pension plan for that person. Once this has taken place there can be a clean break between the partners, which is often the best solution emotionally.

Case study

June and Trevor have decided to go their own ways after 27 years of marriage. Their two children have grown up: one is at university and the other has moved into her own flat. June gave up work to look after the children when they were young and had part-time jobs until they left school. She has no private pension of her own. Trevor has been a member of an occupational money-purchase pension scheme. June would like to stay in the family home but realises she doesn't really need such a large property any more; she does, however, need some pension. They decide to sell the house and split the proceeds so they can both buy flats. June gets a share of Trevor's pension which is paid into her own pension scheme.

What happens to your pension on death?

When you have savings in a pension, it is important to find out what will happen to that money on your death and take steps if necessary to ensure the right people benefit. What happens will depend on a number of factors such as the type of pension scheme you are in, your age and whether or not you have already started drawing an income.

1) State pensions

If you have made more National Insurance contributions towards the basic state pension than your spouse or civil partner, they will be able to inherit your entitlement on your death. This would mean, for example, that if your wife had previously opted to pay the reduced rate married woman's National Insurance contribution and was not entitled to her own basic state pension, she will be able to receive a full basic state pension based on your contributions if she becomes a widow. In the past your widow or widower could also inherit up to 100% of your SERPS or State Second Pension, but this proportion is gradually being reduced and depends on when you reach state pension age. If this occurs after October 2010, your widow, widower or civil partner will only be able to inherit a maximum of 50% of your SERPS or State Second Pension.

2) Salary-related pension schemes

If you die before retirement, your spouse or civil partner will normally receive a pension based on your salary and how long you have been a member of the scheme at the date of your death. Some schemes may give extra pension based on what would have been your full pension at retirement.

If you have no surviving widow, widower or civil partner, the pension may go to your children, if they are under the age of 18 or still in full-time education. Typically the spouse or civil partner's pension will be 50% of what you would have received if you had retired at the time.

If you die after retirement, your spouse will also receive a percentage of your pension, normally a half, which will continue until his or her death.

However, in both cases, if your spouse remarries the pension will normally be stopped. Many widows and widowers for this reason decide to remain unmarried if they meet a new partner. If you die and have no partner or children, no further benefits will be paid out.

3) Money purchase company pension schemes

If you die before retirement, your spouse, partner or children will normally be given the choice of a pension bought with your accumulated pension fund or its value as a lump sum. If you have only been contributing to the scheme for a few years your pension fund may not be worth very much, so additional life insurance is vital. If you die after retirement when your pension is being provided by an annuity, your spouse or partner will normally continue to receive a reduced pension after your death.

4) Stakeholder pensions and personal pensions

If you die before retirement, your pension company will pay the value of your pension savings back to your family. The company has the discretion to choose the beneficiaries because it is acting as a trustee. But it will normally follow your wishes. The money will be free of Inheritance Tax.

Be aware, though, that if you have an old-style personal pension taken out before July 1988, or a Buyout bond (see p. 63), the money will be paid into your estate and could therefore be liable to Inheritance Tax unless you leave it all to your husband, wife or civil partner. You can avoid tax, however, by putting these pensions 'in trust' for your beneficiaries. Your pension company will be able to provide you with a suitable trust form.

If you die after you have started drawing your pension, what happens to your money will depend on how you have decided to take your benefits. If you have bought a pension annuity which only pays an income to you, your pension will stop when you die unless you asked for it to be guaranteed for five or ten years or you have purchased a value-protected

must know

Scotland and Northern Ireland

In Scotland a financial order relating to pensions can be made as part of divorce proceedings. In Northern Ireland a pension sharing order can be made by a court in connection with divorce or annulment proceedings.

annuity (see chapter 5). Then the remaining payments or the balance of your capital will be paid to your estate. If you have a joint life annuity, your pension will continue to be paid until your partner dies.

If you have instead opted to take an 'unsecured income' or income drawdown from your pension savings, your remaining fund can be paid out as a lump sum to your estate, less 35% tax. Alternatively your surviving husband or wife, or civil partner will be able to choose between continuing to take the same type of pension or use the fund to buy an annuity.

If you are over 75 when you die and you had been taking an 'alternatively secured income', your pension fund must be used to provide dependants' pensions if you have any dependants. If you have no dependants, your remaining pension fund can be reallocated, less Inheritance Tax, to anyone you choose to provide pension benefits or it can be paid tax-free to a registered charity of your choice.

Don't forget to tell the trustees

Make sure your pension company knows who you want your pension to go to should you die before retirement age. Most types of pensions, even individual plans such as stakeholder and personal pensions, are written 'in trust' so they can qualify for favourable tax treatment. They are generally overseen by trustees who are responsible for fulfilling all the legal and tax requirements.

One of the responsibilities of the trustees is deciding who should get your pension if you die. Although they will normally pay it to your husband, wife or civil partner, they have discretion. If, for example, you were still legally married/partnered to one person but had been living and supporting another partner for a long period they may be prepared to pay all or part of your pension to that person instead. This discretion has been useful in the past for those in same-sex partnerships, although now there are civil partnerships, a partner's rights are more clear cut.

Whatever your relationship, the best way of ensuring that your pension goes to the right person on your death is to make sure you provide this information to the trustees as 'an expression of wishes'. Forms will normally be provided for this purpose by your pension administrators if you are in a company scheme or your pension company if you have a stakeholder pension or personal pension.

WARNING: If you have an old-style personal pension or retirement annuity taken out pre 1988, the proceeds of your pension will go into your estate when you die where it may be liable to Inheritance Tax. To avoid this, make sure your policy is written in trust for your beneficiaries – ask your pension provider for an appropriate form.

Life insurance and pensions

A top priority in your financial planning if you are part of a couple should be to ensure that neither your partner nor any other dependant suffers from financial hardship after your death. Your pension scheme will help to provide this protection. But will it be enough? The only way of being sure about this is to compare the amount of income your family needs with what they would get after your death.

If you are a member of a salary-related occupational pension scheme, your husband, wife or partner will normally get a lump-sum death-in-service benefit in addition to a regular pension if you die before retirement. The lump sum will normally be between two and four times your annual salary, so if you earn £25,000, for example, your family might get between £50,000 and £100,000. This may sound a lot but if you were the main bread winner this might only tide them over for two to four years.

Unfortunately the closing of many salary-related company pension schemes to new members in recent years means that fewer employees are now getting this life cover through their jobs. Employers who have replaced their company schemes with stakeholder pensions or group personal pension plans for their staff do not normally provide any life cover. And until your pension plan has been running for a reasonable length of time, the benefits your dependants will receive from this type of pension are unlikely to provide adequate financial protection in the event of your premature death.

If your partner is dependent on your income or you have a young family, you will need to take out additional life insurance.

How to get tax relief on your life insurance premiums

It is now possible to get tax relief on your life insurance premiums if you buy pensions term assurance (term assurance is the type of life cover you take out for a specific number of years which pays out if you die during the period but not if you don't – there is no savings element). Just like your pension savings themselves, premiums on this type of life assurance will qualify for tax relief at the same rate that you pay income tax. In theory, this will cut the cost of your insurance premiums by 22% if you are a basic rate taxpayer or by 40% if you pay higher rate tax.

It has been possible to buy pensions term assurance in the past but in recent years the limits on premiums did not make it attractive for most people as it lessened the amount they could invest in their pension. Now that you can get tax relief on contributions of up to 100% of your annual earnings to your pension (subject to a maximum of £215,000 in 2006–07), buying pension term assurance has become attractive again. Although your life insurance premiums will count against your annual limit, this limit is so generous that few people are likely to be saving the maximum in their pension anyway.

But it will still be important to compare the cost of pensions term assurance with ordinary term assurance. Ordinary term assurance has become increasingly competitive in recent years so even after tax relief pensions term assurance may not necessarily be cheaper, particularly for those who pay basic rate tax.

Pensions and wills

It is important for everyone to make a will to make sure that the people you want to get your money when you die will do so. Your pension savings could form a large part of your wealth so you should not forget about them when you are making your will.

However, with most pensions it is the trustees or administrators of the pension scheme who are responsible for deciding who gets your money, so make sure they know your wishes. If you take out any life insurance with your pension, make sure this is also written in trust (your insurance company will tell you how to do this) for your beneficiaries as this will avoid any money being paid into your estate and potentially being liable to Inheritance Tax.

There are three ways to write a will. If you want to DIY, get a form from a stationery shop, fill it out, get it witnessed and tell your executors where to find it in the event of your demise. The second method is to consult a specialist wills company (look in your local phone book) and the third is to consult a solicitor – which may only cost £100 or so, depending on the degree of complexity of your bequests.

Here's what you need to decide to make a will:
• Make a list of your main assets, including your home, savings, investments and pension, and

must know

Your will

Putting a note in your will is not a tax-efficient way to bequeath a pension. Let your pension company know who you want to inherit your fund and find out whether you need to put it in trust.

decide who you want to bequeath them to. Specify percentages of the estate to go to each person, so that you don't need to update your will every time your circumstances change slightly.

• Choose someone to act as your executor – the person who ensures your wishes will be carried out. This can be a family member, friend or your solicitor. Check before you put their name down, because it can be quite a responsibility.

• Decide who would look after children under the age of 18 and/or pets in the event of your demise, and whether you would leave any part of your estate to finance this care.

• You can also include your funeral preferences in a will: burial, cremation, or environmentally friendly woodland burial in a cardboard coffin, for example.

Get two signatories to witness your will (they don't have to read what's in it) then put copies in a safe place. Wills should be reviewed if you get married or divorced, have children, or if the people you have named as heirs or executors die before you.

want to know more?

• For information about keeping your National Insurance contributions up to date, see pages 34-5. If you have taken time off work to be a carer (for children, for example), see the information on page 37 about Home Responsibilities Protection.
• Chapter 7 has advice on how to keep an eye on your pension performance and what to do if you think your fund might be in trouble.
• Chapter 8 looks at different kinds of retirement investments, including ways of making money from your home.

weblinks

• www.opas.org.uk (for independent pension advice)

7 Pensions troubleshooting

No matter how well you have designed your pension and retirement investments, the best-laid plans can always hit a snag. What will happen if your employer goes bust or is taken over? What if your personal pension provider goes to the dogs? To whom can you complain if you feel you have been treated unfairly by a pension company, and how should you deal with it if the unexpected actually happens?

Pensions troubleshooting

Many people have been put off pensions in recent years by scandals such as the Equitable Life problems and company schemes going bust. How can you safeguard your savings?

The basics

The good news is that each time a problem has arisen the Government has tightened the rules to prevent it happening again. And nowadays there are compensation schemes to cover company pensions as well as personal and stakeholder pension plans. So security has improved a lot.

Most of the time, though, things run smoothly and when problems do arise you can get them sorted out quite easily if you know where to go for advice or to make a complaint. This chapter will take you through what to do if things go wrong.

It always pays to be prepared for the worst even if it never happens. Here are some precautionary measures:

• Remember when you first sign up for a pension to keep all the information you are given about the scheme in a safe place for future reference. You may need it in 20 or 30 years' time. If there are any disputes in the future this information could prove invaluable to your case.

• Find out as much as you can about the pension before you join or invest. Don't be shy about asking questions or afraid of sounding stupid. Pensions are complex and you need to be sure you understand what you are getting. Don't assume anything or be fobbed off with generalisations.

• Find out what you will get from your pension if you want to take early retirement, suffer ill health, or die, not just what happens at normal retirement age.
• Check what benefits your partner might receive.
• Ask for all details to be confirmed in writing. When you get written confirmation, read it through and make sure it is what you expected.
• Be sure to look at the regular pension statements you receive to check that the promises you were made are being delivered.
• Tell your partner where to find details about your pension in the event of your death.

Problems with your employer's final salary scheme

Occupational pension schemes are often in the news nowadays. Most of the press articles concern salary-related pension schemes, many of which are currently in 'deficit' – this means the value of the investments in the pension fund does not meet the cost of all the pensions promised to employees and ex-employees. As a consequence, many employers have closed down their schemes to new employees and some have stopped existing employees building up further pension benefits too. Others are modifying their schemes to make them less costly.

Even more worrying for some pension scheme members is the prospect of their employer being taken over or going out of business. So what do these developments mean if you are a pension scheme member and how are you protected if the worst happens and your company goes bust?

Pension fund deficits. Most of the UK's private companies with salary-related pension schemes

must know

Just ask...

If you would like to know more about the financial state of your company pension ask your human resources department who it is that you need to contact. They may be able to help or will put you in touch with the pension scheme administrators. If you have any trouble getting information or don't understand the implications, contact the Pensions Advisory Service at www.opas .org.uk or tel: 0845 601 2923.

now have pension deficits, mainly due to the poor stockmarket conditions of a few years ago which saw the value of their investments plummet. This problem has been combined with the fact that people are living longer, so pension schemes are having to pay out pensions for longer.

When a deficit occurs the employer is responsible for putting extra money into the scheme. The Pensions Regulator, the Government's watchdog responsible for the UK's occupational pensions, is currently working with employers on their plans for making up these deficits.

However, such is the size of the deficits it may take some companies 10 years or more to plug the gaps in their pension schemes. If you are a member of a scheme in deficit, where does this leave you? If you are worried about putting in more savings, pouring good money after bad, what are your options?

• Stopping your pension contributions is not a good idea because it means that you will miss out on the contributions your employer is still obliged to make.

• Withdrawing your existing pension savings in the form of a transfer value will mean you will get significantly less than the true value of your pension benefits as the pension fund trustees will reduce them in line with the deficit to ensure remaining members do not suffer. This means that if your scheme is, say, 30% underfunded your transfer value will be 30% less than it should be.

• If your employer's business is otherwise in sound financial health, the deficit will gradually be made up and the pension scheme will be obliged to deliver on its pension promises to you when you get to retirement.

• If you think there is a problem with your pension fund that the authorities may not be aware of you can contact the Pensions Regulator in confidence and ask staff to look into it.

• But even if the worst did happen and your company went bust leaving the scheme in deficit, you are nowadays covered by the Pension Protection Fund (see p.144).

Changes to your scheme. If your employer decides to modify an occupational pension scheme, there is little you can do about it. Past pension promises must be honoured but future benefits can be changed. Changes that have been adopted by some employers in order to reduce their future pension costs include:
• asking employees to make extra contributions if they want to receive the same pension benefits in future
• asking employees to work extra years
• switching the basis on which the pension is calculated from a final salary to a career average scheme.

While these measures may leave you somewhat worse off than you would have been before, you are still likely to get a better deal than you would in a money-purchase company pension or a personal pension or stakeholder pension where there is much less certainty about future benefits and you are taking all the investment risk yourself. And for some people who would like to work part-time in the final years of their working life and therefore earn less, a career-average pension scheme could actually produce better results for them than a final salary scheme.

Case study

Jack had built up a pension of £15,000 with his ex-employer. He has recently left the company and is concerned about its future and worried what will happen to his pension if it goes to the wall. He has enquired about taking a transfer value but as the pension scheme is in deficit he would get 25% less than his pension is really worth. He is thinking about cutting his losses and taking the transfer value anyway but when his financial adviser points out that 90% of his pension is covered by the Pension Protection Fund he decides to leave it where it is.

Takeovers, mergers and management buyouts.
When the company you work for is taken over, it can be a worrying time. Your main concern is likely to be for your job, but your pension will come a close second. For those nearing retirement it is likely to be at the top of their list of priorities.

Nowadays, though, this should not make any difference to your pension. Directors are not allowed to sell their companies in order to get out of putting more money into the pensions scheme.

Any professional advisers involved in the transaction are expected to inform the Pensions Regulator if they suspect this to be the case. The Regulator can issue warnings to a company's owners anywhere in the world requiring them to meet their obligations, although their ability to enforce these orders outside the UK has yet to be tested in court.

Closure of a salary-related pension scheme.
When a salary-related pension scheme is closed this will not affect the pension you have already built up – the company is still obliged to honour its promises. If it wants to wind the scheme up altogether, it will have to ensure there is enough in the scheme to buy you a deferred pension with an insurance company which matches what you would have received from the company scheme.

The Pension Protection Fund

If the worst comes to the worst and your employer goes bust leaving its salary-related pension scheme in deficit, the Pension Protection Fund will provide a safety net.

The Fund was set up by the Government in April 2005 after several firms closed down and employees lost all their pension savings. However, the money does not come from the Government, which has made it clear taxpayers will not be called on to bail out failing pension funds.

The Pension Protection Fund covers all employees who are in salary-related pension schemes. The money in the Fund, which pays compensation to those who lose their savings, comes from other salary-related pension schemes. Any money left in the company's own pension fund will also be used to help pay compensation.

Before deciding on compensation, the Pension Protection Fund will try to find out whether the scheme can be rescued, maybe by another company taking over the employer and assuming responsibility for the pension scheme. The investments in the fund will also be checked to see if there is enough to pay compensation equal to that provided by the Fund. If not the Pension Protection Fund will take over and arrange for compensation to be paid to members.

There are two levels of compensation:

1) **For existing pensioners.** Anyone who has reached their scheme's normal retirement age, or is already receiving a pension, say due to ill health, will receive 100% compensation so they will get their full pension. If part of their pension relates to service since April 1997, that part will also continue to rise in line with the Retail Prices Index up to a maximum of 2.5% per year.

2) **For those yet to retire.** If you are below your scheme's normal retirement age you will normally receive 90% of the pension due to you at the time your employer becomes insolvent. Someone entitled

to a pension of £5,000, for example, would get 90% of that amount – i.e., £4,500. But compensation is capped at £25,000 a year at age 65.

Between the point at which compensation is agreed and when the pension is payable at your normal retirement age, it will be revalued in line with the Retail Prices Index up to a maximum of 5% per year. Once in payment, inflation-related increases will also be given for service after April 1997 up to a maximum of 2.5% per year.

For most employees, the Pension Protection Fund will provide a good safety net unless they have built up more than £25,000 a year of pension. People in this situation who have reason to believe their employer may go bust should seek independent financial advice as soon as possible.

Where to go if you have pension problems

Even if the worst never happens, other problems can arise with your pension. There are various organisations that can help and advise you and, if necessary, award you compensation depending on the type of pension you have. But firstly you will need to try to resolve the problems yourself.

If you belong to a private company's occupational final salary or money purchase scheme (as opposed to a group personal pension or stakeholder scheme) you will normally need to contact the trustees if you have a problem. Your human resources department can provide you with contact details. If you work in the public sector, it is slightly different. You will need to contact the scheme authorities, such as the NHS Pensions Agency or Teachers' Pensions.

must know

More about the PPF

For more details on the Pension Protection Fund visit its website at www.pensionprotection fund.org.uk or tel: 0845 600 2541.

It is normally better to put your problem in writing. Always keep a copy of the correspondence. Try to keep your letter brief and to the point, stating the problem concisely and what you believe the solution to be. If they want more details from you, they can ask. If it is urgent and you feel it would be quicker to use the telephone, remember to make notes of your conversation. It is still a good idea to follow up your call up with a letter to make sure no misunderstandings have arisen.

If you are not satisfied with the response from your pension provider, contact the Pensions Advisory Service, which is a free service staffed by advisers who used to work in the pensions industry. One of these advisers will gather all the relevant information from you and your pension administrator and will then look at the details of your situation and advise you whether you have a case or not. If not, the reason will be explained to you. If it is thought you do have a case, the adviser will help you resolve the matter. This may result in a compromise but if you are still not satisfied you will be able to take your complaint to the Pensions Ombudsman. Before you go to the Ombudsman, though, you must use your pension scheme's 'internal dispute resolution procedure' which every scheme must offer. Your adviser from the Pensions Advisory Service can help you through this process, or you can act alone or with the help of someone else, such as a friend or union official. Widows or widowers, or surviving civil partners or dependants can represent pension scheme members after their death. If all else fails, you can take your case to the Pensions Ombudsman (see box, right, for contact details).

Personal pension/stakeholder pension problems

It is not only company pension funds that have suffered from the poor stockmarket conditions of a few years ago – your personal pension or stakeholder pension may not have performed as well as you hoped either.

Bonuses on many 'with profits' pension plans have not been as good as companies predicted. Some companies have closed their 'with profits' funds or sold them on to other companies. In both cases, the investment mix in the funds has often been changed so that less is now being invested in shares. This is one of the reasons that it is important to review your pension policies regularly.

Another point to bear in mind if you have a personal pension plan which was taken out before stakeholder pensions were introduced in 2001 is that the charges may still be considerably higher than they are on plans being taken out today. This can also hold performance back.

To find out how the charges on your plan compare, ask your existing pension provider for an up-to-date projection of the pension you would get from your current savings and then ask a stakeholder pension company for an illustration based on the same amount of saving. They all have to assume the same amount of investment growth so the one with the highest projection will have the lowest level of charges.

If you have an underperforming personal pension or stakeholder pension or an old plan with high charges, it may be worth considering transferring your savings to a new pension provider. However, if you have an old-style personal pension you will need to check the potential transfer penalties and whether your pension includes a guaranteed annuity rate before going ahead.

Seek independent financial advice if you are unsure about reviewing your existing pensions. You may have to pay a fee but it will almost certainly be worth it.

How well is your pension company performing?

If you want to find out how your pension company rates in terms of its pension performance, look at the surveys of past performance published regularly in *Money Management* magazine – available at newsagents or tel: 020 8606 7545. *Money Management* asks all companies that have offered personal pensions in the past for their figures. So if your company has not supplied its figures to the magazine, it is a fair assumption that it is not very proud of its performance. Past performance is of course no guide to the future but the *Money Management* surveys highlight those doing consistently well and those doing consistently badly. If you are unsure about how good your existing pension plans are, seek independent financial advice.

If you have a personal pension or stakeholder pension – even if you signed up to it through your employer and contributions are being taken direct from your pay – your contract will be with the pension company so you will need to direct any queries or complaints to them. If you can't resolve it through normal customer services, contact the firm's Compliance Officer.

It is normally best to put your problem in writing. Always keep a copy of the correspondence. Try to keep your letter brief and to the point, stating the problem and what you believe the solution to be. If they want more details from you, they can ask. If it is urgent and you feel it would be quicker to use the telephone, remember to make notes of your conversation. It is still advisable to follow up your call with a letter to make sure no misunderstandings have arisen. If you are unable to resolve matters this way, it is a good idea to approach the Pensions

Advisory Service for advice about which organisation you should complain to next. If your complaint mainly concerns the advice you were given about your pension or the sales or marketing side of the process, you will be pointed in the direction of the Financial Ombudsman Service (FOS) (see opposite).

If your complaint mainly concerns the operation of the scheme, the Pensions Advisory Service will ask you for all the relevant documents and correspondence. Its advisers can deal directly with your pension provider and may be able to resolve matters for you. If not and they tell you that you have a case, you can take your complaint to the Pensions Ombudsman (see below).

Case study
When Peter was 63, he decided to give his personal pension a final boost with a lump sum investment. He made it clear to his financial adviser that he did not want to invest it anywhere too risky as he was going to retire in two years' time. The adviser suggested an index tracker fund that had gone down in value by the time Peter retired. Peter felt he had been sold an unsuitable investment and complained to the Financial Ombudsman Service, which upheld his complaint and awarded him compensation.

The Pensions Ombudsman
The Pensions Ombudsman deals with complaints about 'maladministration' by occupational pension schemes, personal pension plans and stakeholder schemes. Maladministration covers problems such as incompetence and delay.

Before contacting the Ombudsman you must already have complained to your pension trustees or pension provider or whomever you consider to be at fault. Nowadays they must all have procedures for dealing with complaints. If this does not help, you must complain to the Ombudsman within three years of the reason for your complaint occurring. After hearing the facts, the Ombudsman will decide whether a case falls within his jurisdiction.

Complaints to the Pensions Ombudsman must be made in writing so you will need to complete a form which you can get from the Ombudsman's office or download from the website. One of the Ombudsman's investigators will then tell you whether your complaint can be looked at or not. If it is going to be examined, the necessary papers will be requested and the body approached that you are complaining about. The process of looking into a pension complaint can take quite a while, sometimes more than a year. If the Ombudsman finds in your favour, his decision will be aimed at putting you in the position you should have been in if maladministration had not occurred. The Ombudsman's decision is final and can only be disputed on a point of law.

The Financial Ombudsman Service

If you have a problem with your personal pension or stakeholder pension scheme, such as how it was sold to you or the advice you were given, the Financial Ombudsman Service may be able to sort out the matter for you and get you compensation. But it does not deal with investment-related complaints unless you can show you were not warned about the investment risks involved.

Before you take your complaint to the Financial Ombudsman, you will have to show that you have given the company that sold you the pension a chance to put things right. So write to the company, heading your letter 'complaint', give a brief outline of the facts, state the problem and what you regard the solution to be. Send copies, not originals, of relevant documents. Keep a copy of the correspondence for reference. If you are unhappy with the outcome, check with the company that it has given you

must know

State pensions

You can get general advice on state pensions from the Pensions Advisory Service or the Pensions Service, tel: 0845 606 0265; but if you have a specific complaint you should deal with your local Department of Work and Pensions office, or contact the central pensions department: The Pension Service, Tyneview Park Whitley Benton Newcastle-upon-Tyne NE98 1BA.

its 'final response' and you can then complain to the Ombudsman. If the company does not respond within eight weeks of your complaint, you can also go to the Ombudsman.

You must complain to the Ombudsman within six months of the company's final response letter. The Ombudsman will then look into your complaint and can tell the firm to make good your losses up to £100,000. The decision by the Financial Ombudsman Service is binding on the firm but not on you so you can still take the matter to court if you are disappointed with the Ombudsman's verdict.

What happens if your pension company goes bust?

This should never happen nowadays if the city watchdog, the Financial Services Authority (FSA), is doing its job property, as it is meant to check pension companies' financial strength regularly. If the worst did come to the worst, the Financial Services Compensation Scheme would come into effect. This would pay you back 100% of the first £2,000 in your pension plan and 90% of its remaining value.

Strictly personal

Some problems with pensions may arise for personal reasons, such as ill health or bankruptcy. Here are some suggestions for dealing with such eventualities.

Ill health

If you are unable to work due to ill health or disability, you may be eligible for an ill-health pension if you are a member of an occupational pension scheme. This won't be the case if you are paying into a group personal pension or stakeholder scheme, although your employer may have a separate arrangement called an 'income protection scheme' with an insurance company, which will pay you some income while you are off sick. If you have a personal pension or stakeholder pension and you become seriously ill you may be able to draw on your benefits earlier than usual. But you will need to discuss this with your pension provider and medical evidence will be required.

Even getting an ill health early retirement pension from an occupational pension scheme is no longer as easy as it used to be in the days when company pension schemes had plenty of resources. Nowadays, pension schemes have much more rigorous procedures for deciding whether someone qualifies for an ill health pension. It will also depend on your pension scheme's rules. It may be useful to get a copy of the rules so you know where you stand.

The rules may state that you are only eligible for an ill-health pension if you are unable to do any job at all, for any employer, and not just because you are unable to do your usual job. Your pension trustees are also unlikely to take your GP's word for it that you are unable to work, and the fact that you are receiving state disability benefit may also not be sufficient. Even if you are seeing a specialist, they will probably ask you to see a specialist of their choice. You may even be asked to pay for this medical report yourself.

In many cases, the payment of an ill-health pension is entirely at the discretion of the pension trustees, or even your employer. If they decide against your claim, it will only be possible to

must know

Income protection insurance

If you are self-employed or your employer does not provide sick pay, income protection insurance that will cover periods when you are too ill to work is a good investment. You will get it cheaper if you can wait for three or even six months after the onset of illness before payments kick in.

challenge them if they have behaved unreasonably. But they should give you a reason for their decision and if they do not, or you feel the explanation is unsatisfactory, you should contact the Pensions Advisory Service.

If you are accepted for an ill-health pension, the pension you get will be based on your current entitlement but in some more generous schemes it will be enhanced to the level it would have been at your normal retirement age.

With a money-purchase occupational pension or a personal pension or stakeholder scheme, although in theory a pension could be drawn early in the event of serious ill health in practice this is usually not practical. There may not be enough money in your pension pot and annuity rates will be low if you are a long way off normal retirement age.

If you are lucky your employer may have group income protection insurance instead. In this case, you will continue to be paid and your employer will reclaim the money from the insurance company. However, these payments may only continue for up to five years rather than until retirement. The best solution is to find out what your employer will provide if you suffer long-term ill health, and then take out your own income protection insurance to top up the cover.

Bankruptcy

An increasing number of people with debt problems are resorting to bankruptcy as a way out. If you are already drawing a pension, it will be counted as part of your income in assessing your ability to repay your creditors. But if you are below retirement age,

must know

Unemployment

If you are laid off and have a period when you can't make your normal contributions, write to your pension company and let them know what's happened if you have a personal pension. If you just stop paying, they may make your pension 'paid up' and charge you an administration fee. If you have a stakeholder pension you don't have to worry as you cannot be penalised for stopping your contributions.

your pension savings will not be affected. However, if you have deliberately ploughed money into your pension because you knew you were about to become bankrupt, your scheme may well have to pay it back to help meet your debts. Judges tend to have suspicious minds.

want to know more?

• You may wish to take out some other forms of investment besides a pension for extra cash in your retirement or to cushion yourself against your pension fund underperforming. Chapter 8 discusses some of the best products to put in your investment portfolio.
• There is a glossary of terms used in this book on pages 184-5, and a full listing of useful addresses on pages 188-9.

weblinks

• www.pension protectionfund.org.uk
• www.pensions-ombudsman.org.uk
• www.financial-ombudsman.org.uk
• www.opas.org.uk

8 Saving for retirement outside a pension

Even if pensions are the bread and butter of your retirement income, it's good to have some other types of investment to buy treats and provide an emergency safety net. This chapter outlines the advantages and the pitfalls of different savings and investment plans, from buy-to-let property through to guaranteed income bonds, and advises on equity release and schemes for paying for care, if necessary.

Saving for retirement outside a pension

A pension is not the only way to save for retirement. There are plenty of other types of savings and investments that can be used to build a retirement nest egg.

must know

Beware!

You may notice ads in the paper offering incredible returns on investments, such as 300% return on your money after two years. Or perhaps you get a phone call inviting you to invest in a sure-fire winning scheme. Remember the rule that if it sounds too good to be true, that's because it is. Chances are you would never see your money again!

Where to invest your savings

You might like to build up a range of alternative savings and investments as well as your pension, to give you funds to dip into for luxuries. Or you might be looking for a way to invest a lump sum received on retirement. Either way, there is a variety of investments that can be used to pay you a regular income.

If you want to make some savings outside a pension, you will need a 'before' and 'after' retirement investment strategy. This chapter will look at your main savings and investment choices, but there is a checklist opposite of factors to consider before you start; think about them carefully.

The main reasons for saving for retirement through a pension are the tax advantages. The most tempting is the income tax relief that is given on your savings, which helps you to build up your pension fund more quickly than if you were saving the same amount of money elsewhere. In return for these tax concessions there are restrictions on when and how you can get at your money – but having savings locked away until retirement may be no bad thing. It means you won't be able to dip into them early. Most people, however, would like a bit of flexibility

Checklist for retirement saving and investing

Before retirement

1) Remember your main aim is to build up your savings, so concentrate on investments where your capital is likely to grow.

2) Work out how many years you have until your planned retirement age, since this will affect your savings choices:
- over 10 years – consider shares or property
- under 5 years – savings accounts are lower risk.

3) Don't put all your eggs in one basket – however sound an investment may seem, pouring all your savings into one area is a high-risk strategy.

4) Look for tax-efficient savings and investments, so your money can grow faster.

5) Review your investments regularly to make sure they are still giving competitive returns.

At or after retirement

1) List all your savings and investments. If you are a couple, look at dividing your savings between you to make the most of your tax allowances.

2) Consider your cash needs for your retirement – such as any major planned expenditure, and how much monthly income you will need.

3) Keep cash for immediate spending needs in a savings account.

4) When investing for income, think about the long term. Remember your retirement may last 20 years, and you need to think of ways of keeping up with rising prices.

5) Think of getting money out of your home through 'equity release' as a last rather than a first resort – it's an expensive way of getting cash (see page 162).

and some remain unconvinced that pensions are such a good idea despite the tax perks. In recent years there has been a growing perception that the ideal investment for retirement is buying property to let rather than going for the pension.

As always, the best solution for most people is to adopt a mixture of strategies – splitting your spare cash between a pension and other types of savings and not putting all your bets on any one type of investment, since this can end in disaster. Look for the most tax-efficient ways of saving, but don't let saving tax become an end in itself. When you get to retirement, it is also good idea to try and spread your savings around.

Investing in property

In recent years, investing in property has been seen as one of the best alternatives to saving in a pension. People have watched their own homes shoot up in value and some have made a lot of money out of buying property and letting it out. But even this apparently sure-fire investment has its snags. The property market and rental incomes are not always as predictable as some people believe, so it is not a wise idea to have property as your only investment.

As a result of rapidly rising house prices in recent years, many homeowners now regard the property they live in as not just a home but an investment as well, and one that will help see them through their retirement. Money spent on home improvements is seen as a way of increasing the value of this investment. But the problem with placing too much emphasis on your home as an investment is that you will have to find a way of releasing the capital when you get to retirement.

Downsizing

The best way of unlocking the value from your home when you stop working is by downsizing – moving to a smaller property. Many people are still living in a family-sized home when they reach retirement even though their children have left. So their property is probably larger than they really need anyway. Trading down to a smaller, cheaper property will mean having to pay all the usual moving costs such as estate agents' fees, legal fees and stamp duty. But it will have a number of financial benefits.

Besides enabling you to release capital you can invest for income, moving to a smaller property will often mean lower maintenance and heating costs and a lower council tax bill, so your outgoings will go down, giving you more of your existing income to spend on other things.

The main problem with this approach is that many of us get emotionally attached to our homes if we have lived there for many years. You may have good, supportive neighbours, and finding a suitable smaller property in the immediate vicinity may be difficult. So be realistic. If you don't think you will be able to wrench yourself away from your home or neighbour-hood, make bigger efforts to boost your pension or save elsewhere.

If you are serious about cashing in on your home as an investment, work out what proportion of its value you regard as an investment. In other words, if you sold it, roughly how much would you have left after you had bought yourself a cheaper property? Then when you are considering where your money is currently invested, you should list this amount under property investment. This will help you to plan your other savings better. If a large chunk of your home is earmarked as an investment, the 'not putting all your eggs in one basket' rule applies. This means the rest of your savings should go into other types of investments (see pages 169–73).

(see pages 169–73)

must know

Property development

Some tips: don't think you know how to do it because you've watched all those makeover shows on TV. Building work almost invariably comes in over budget and it can be tricky keeping it on schedule because the unexpected will happen. Leave a generous contingency budget to cover extra costs, including a few extra months' mortgage payments if the property doesn't sell as quickly as you had hoped.

You might find you can't face selling your home. If so, there may be other ways you can get money out of your property.

Rent-a-room

If you have a spare room, taking in lodgers such as foreign students learning English could be quite a fun way of making money out of your property. The main advantage is that there is a special rent-a-room tax allowance under which the first £4,520 of income each tax year from letting a room (or rooms) in your home is tax-free. If you get more than the tax-exempt amount from letting rooms you will have to pay tax on the excess.

Borrowing money from your family

If you are hoping eventually to pass on your home to your children, it is worth discussing your options with them. They may be able to give you a loan against the property. If you decide to do this you will need to go to a lawyer so that a proper legal agreement can be drawn up. This way everybody will know exactly where they stand, and if you do eventually need long-term care and you are means tested, it will be clear that part of the proceeds of your house must be used to repay the debt to your children.

Equity release

Equity release schemes allow you to take money out of your home and go on living there without having to make any repayments. The debt doesn't have to be paid back until your property is sold – usually when you die or need to move into long-term care. They may sound ideal but they are very expensive.

must know

Rental contracts

Remember that being a landlord can involve a lot of hassle. You'll have to collect the rent, chase late- or non-payers and handle calls at 4am when the pipes burst. If you go through an agency, they will take the strain but will charge a percentage of the rental income.

Even if you only take out a small part of the market value of your home, by the time you die the loan is likely to have grown enormously and there may be little or no spare capital left in your home. If you don't have children or others you want to pass money on to, this may not bother you. But you will need to look carefully at your options for moving in the future.

If you are part of a couple you will need to consider the situation of your surviving partner who may want to move to sheltered accommodation after you have died and be unable to do so if an equity release scheme is in place.

Equity release should always be regarded as a last resort after you have looked into all other ways of improving your cash position.

If you do decide to go ahead, make sure you understand exactly the risks involved.

There are two main types of scheme – lifetime mortgages and home reversion schemes. The minimum age at which they can be taken out is typically either 60 or 65.

1) Lifetime mortgages. The amount you can borrow under these schemes depends on your age. The older you are the more you can borrow but most schemes limit loans to a maximum of 40%–50% of your property value.

The main difference from an ordinary mortgage is that you don't have to make any regular repayments. Instead the interest on the loan is added to your outstanding debt monthly or annually to be repaid when the house is sold. This may sound harmless enough, but it has a snowball effect – the loan gets larger and larger and the interest payments get bigger and bigger. After ten years the amount you

must know

What is rolled-up interest?

Because the interest charged is added to the debt, in the second month you will be paying interest on the interest for the first month; in the third month, you will pay interest on the interest for the first and second months. This is known as rolled-up interest, and it explains why your debt can increase so quickly when you take out this kind of loan.

owe can double. At 7%, for example, a £50,000 loan on a £200,000 property could turn into a debt of nearly £200,000 after 20 years.

Interest rates on lifetime mortgages are normally higher than ordinary mortgage rates and are usually fixed at the outset, so you are protected against future increases but you won't benefit if rates go down. And there are usually steep redemption penalties to stop you moving to a cheaper loan elsewhere.

When a mortgage is set up you may be offered a lump sum immediately which you can use for any purpose. As an alternative, a growing number of lenders now allow you to draw down the money gradually as a series of lump sums or a monthly income. If you don't need the lump sum for a particular purpose, choosing a drawdown arrangement will help to keep the cost down because you will only be accumulating interest on the amounts you have actually borrowed.

There will be a range of fees to pay when you set up your loan, including an application fee, arrangement fee, valuation fee and legal fees. Your adviser will normally receive commission of between 1% and 2% of the amount you borrow from the lender.

Potential cost of an equity release lifetime mortgage

Amount you will owe if you take a £50,000 loan against your home with rolled-up interest

Interest Rate	6%	7%	8%
After 5 Years	66,900	70,150	73,450
After 10 Years	89,550	98,350	107,950
After 20 Years	160,350	193,500	233,050

2) **Home reversions**. With these schemes you sell all or part of your property to the reversion company in return for a lump sum or in some cases a lifetime income. Even if you sell all your home, you still have the right to live in the property for the rest of your life. You don't have to pay any rent but you must still maintain the property in good condition.

Safe home income plans

If you decide to go ahead with an equity release scheme, make sure you deal with a company which is a member of the Safe Home Income Plans Association (SHIP). SHIP members must sign up to a code of practice covering their dealings with homeowners. Under the code members must:

• Provide a fair, simple and complete presentation of their plans. This must include all costs, the position on moving, the tax situation and the effect of changes in house values.

• Ensure that the client's legal work is performed by a solicitor of his or her choice. The solicitor must be provided with full details of the benefits the client will receive prior to the completion of the plan. The solicitor must sign a certificate confirming that the scheme has been fully explained to the client.

• This certificate will also state clearly the cost to the householder and his or her estate and will state whether part or all of the property is being sold.

The plans of SHIP members also include important safeguards:

• They carry a 'no negative equity' guarantee, which means you will never owe more than the value of your home. This is particularly important with roll-up plans (where the interest is added to your mortgage) as your debt could otherwise eventually exceed the value of your home.

• You have the right to live in your property for life even if you have sold all your interest or your debt eventually matches the value of your home.

• You will have the freedom to move to suitable alternative property without financial penalties – but check what your provider deems to be 'suitable'.

• You will be guaranteed a cash sum or regular income payments. A list of SHIP members can be found at www.ship-ltd.org.

Don't expect to get anywhere near the market value of your home if you sell it under a home reversion scheme. You might typically get around 40% of its value if you are aged 65. The other 60% is the cost of getting the money early. This means if your house is worth £200,000 and you sell half of it, market value £100,000, you will receive £40,000. The exact amount will depend on your age and sex – the older you are the more you will get because the company does not expect to have to wait so long for its money.

Case study

Sarah, 72, is considering equity release to pay for some necessary maintenance to her home and to give her some extra spending money. She is considering borrowing £50,000 at a fixed rate of 6.5% against her £250,000 house. But when she discovers that in 15 years time the debt could stand at over half the value of her house, she decides to sell up and buy a cheaper modern flat instead. This way her maintenance costs will be lower and she will have some money in the bank.

When your house is sold if you go into long-term care or die, the reversion company has a right to the full value of its share, even if the price has risen significantly since you originally completed the deal. So if your £200,000 property is now worth £300,000, the reversion company will take £150,000 in repayment for its £40,000 loan.

The final cost of a home reversion scheme will therefore be largely determined by the movement of house prices. It could be more or less expensive than a mortgage scheme, but if you don't sell the whole house at least you will know exactly what proportion will go to your beneficiaries.

When you first set up the scheme there will be valuation and legal fees to pay. Your adviser will receive commission of up to 3% of the capital you take out of your property. Home reversion schemes should be approached with even more care than mortgage schemes as they are not yet regulated by the City watchdog, the Financial Services Authority (FSA).

Buy to let

If you have not yet reached retirement, you might fancy the idea of buying another property as a way of investing for retirement. Increasing house prices have made residential property a source of capital growth in recent years, and rents are seen as a good way of generating income in retirement. But neither is guaranteed.

Prospective property buyers should remember that house prices can go down as well as up. The table below shows how much they have fluctuated in the last 20 years. In 1988, for example, they rose by 34% while in 1992, they fell back 8%. Returns from rents can also be quite modest. Over five years to the end of 2005, the average rental return was 4.61% according to the Association of Residential Letting Agents.

On the next pages you will find some of the things you need to consider, if you are planning to buy to let.

Houses price movements are not always upwards

1986	+13.5%	1996	+7.4%
1987	+15.5%	1997	+5.4%
1988	+34.0%	1998	+5.5%
1989	+5.1%	1999	+11.5%
1990	0.0%	2000	+5.7%
1991	-2.4%	2001	+11.7%
1992	-8.3%	2002	+26.4%
1993	+1.6%	2003	+15.4%
1994	-0.8%	2004	+15.1%
1995	-1.5%	2005	+5.1%

Source: Halifax

Buy-to-let mortgages. Even if you have enough cash to buy a property outright, getting a loan is often a good idea as you can offset the interest on your loan against the rent you receive so you will pay less income tax. Buy-to-let loans have become cheaper in recent years, but they generally have higher rates than ordinary residential mortgages. Before you can borrow, you will need enough cash to pay a deposit of 15% to 25% of the price, as the maximum buy-to-let loan is 75% to 85% of the property value.

In order to decide how much they will lend you, most lenders will take your potential rental income into account, but the amount you get in rent will normally have to be at least 25% higher than your mortgage repayments. Lenders may not be willing to lend on all types of property or allow all types of tenants, so check this beforehand. For example, they may not lend on new-build flats or student, local authority or holiday lets.

Rental income. Bear in mind your rental income is not guaranteed. You must be prepared for gaps between tenants – voids – when your income may dry up completely for a few months. And you may have to deal with the occasional non-paying tenant. So you will need to be sure you are able to repay your mortgage from other sources during these periods, or have other pensions and savings income you can fall back on if you are retired.

In recent years, the increasing amount of property to let has put downward pressure on rents in some areas, so you could actually find your rental income falling rather than rising. Also remember that you will need to keep back some money to cover the cost of maintenance and repairs to the property. If you employ a letting agent to find your tenants and manage your property, this additional cost will come out of your rental income.

Tax. You will have to pay income tax on the rent you receive from your property and when you come to sell it you will have to pay capital gains tax on any profit you make (unlike your own home where any gains are free of tax).

Other ways to increase your retirement savings

When considering other ways of boosting your retirement savings, try to opt for tax-efficient options first. Your timescale will also be an important consideration. The closer you are to retirement, the less risk you may want to take with your money.

Tax free savings

Individual Savings Accounts (ISAs). ISAs are one of the most popular ways of making extra savings for retirement because they are tax-efficient and very flexible. Up to £7,000 per tax year can invested in ISAs, either in a lump sum or by regular savings starting at around £20 per month. You can either split your allowance, putting up to £3,000 into a mini-cash ISA, and up to £4,000 into a mini stocks and shares ISA, normally containing stockmarket related investments, or you could put the full £7,000 into a maxi stocks and shares ISA.

Mini cash ISAs. A good starting-point for all savers, they are like ordinary savings accounts but the interest is tax-free. Your capital is secure so they can form a firm foundation for your savings. Search out

must know

Before you buy a property to let

If you are interested in buying property to let, it is a good idea to speak to a local letting agent first to find out what kind of property is in most demand among local tenants. Contact the Association of Residential Letting Agents (ARLA) for details of agents in your area. Other useful information for prospective landlords can be found on its website www.arla.co.uk, tel: 0845 3455752.

the top-paying accounts and review them regularly to make sure you are still getting the best rate.

Stocks and shares ISAs. These can generally go down as well as up in value, but there are many different types of investment funds to choose from and some are less risky than others. In any case taking risks can pay off if you have 10 years or more until retirement. Historically shares have produced better returns over the long term than other types of investments. Index tracker funds are the cheapest option if you want to invest in the stockmarket. They buy the shares that make up the stockmarket indices such as the FTSE 100. It means you don't have to worry about picking the best-managed funds.

But share prices can fluctuate, so if you want your savings to grow more smoothly the best approach is to build up a mixture of different types of funds so that you have a balance. You can buy funds investing in bonds (loans to governments and companies), which tend to perform well when shares are underperforming, and in commercial property, which will give you extra diversity.

ISAs generally have no fixed investment term, so you can withdraw your money at any time – although you should have a time horizon of at least five or ten years to get the best returns. With some ISA products, such as 'capital protected' ISAs, there is a specified term, which means there could be a penalty for early withdrawal.

National Savings and Investments. National Savings Certificates are completely secure investments as they are backed by the Government. The returns are guaranteed and tax-free. You have the choice of fixed-rate certificates which pay a

must know

Getting Government backing

Details of National Savings & Investments products can be obtained from post offices (pick up leaflets) or by going to www.nsandi.co.uk. Products can be bought by post, by telephone at 0500 500 000 or online.

guaranteed rate of interest over either a two- or a five-year term, or index-linked certificates which run for three or five years where the returns rise in line with the Retail Price Index with a modest amount of added interest on top. Index-linked certificates are the best option if you would like complete certainty, as they are one of the few investments that are absolutely guaranteed to beat inflation. Between £100 and £15,000 can be invested in each type of certificate each time a new issue is brought out.

Premium Bonds should not form a major part of your retirement planning. You could put some of your cash savings into them, but bear in mind that though the monetary value of your capital is secure its value will be gradually eroded by inflation unless you win a prize. For a stake of between £100 and £30,000 you get the chance to win two £1 million monthly jackpots plus a variety of smaller prizes, which are tax-free. However, the odds on winning are very low. In theory, if you invest the maximum amount, you could get regular prizes equivalent to the prize fund interest but this is still less than you would get from a competitive savings account and there is no guarantee that you will get these prizes. Only consider premium bonds for a small part (if any) of your savings.

Tax-exempt friendly society plans are life-insurance policies with a minimum term of 10 years. Your savings are normally invested in tax-free with profits or managed funds and the policy proceeds are tax-free. The premiums are limited to a maximum of £25 per month but the charges can be relatively high, which can offset the tax advantages. You will be penalised if policies are cashed in early.

must know

Shopping around

• For details of best buy Mini cash ISAs go to www.moneyfacts.co.uk or www.moneynet.co.uk.
• Spread your Stocks and Shares ISA investments across several funds using a fund supermarket such as Fundsnetwork, www.fundsnetwork.co.uk.
• To find which fund managers are most highly rated go to www.citywire .co.uk, or www.best invest.co.uk
• For fund performance information go to www.trustnet.co.uk or www.morningstar.co.uk
• For ISA manager contact details telephone the Investment Management Association (IMA) on 020 7831 0898, www.invest mentuk.org or the Association of Investment Trust Companies (AITC) on 0800 707 707, www.aitc .co.uk .
• If you are not sure which ISA is right for you, seek independent advice; go to www.unbiased.co.uk, or call 0800 085 3250 for a list of advisers in your area.

must know

**Discounted ISAs
and investment
funds**

If you know which funds
you want, pay a reduced
initial charge by using a
discount broker such as
Bestinvest, tel: 020 7189
9999, www.bestinvest
.co.uk; Chartwell tel:
01225 446556,
www.chartwell-
investment.co.uk; or
Financial Discounts
Direct tel: 0500 498
477, www.financial-
discount.co.uk.

Venture Capital Trusts (VCTs) are very high risk.
They are one of the few investments other than
pensions where you get income tax relief on your
savings. The Enterprise Investment Scheme (EIS) is a
similar type of investment. The aim of both schemes
is to encourage investors to back small businesses.
The difference is that VCTs hold portfolios of shares
in unquoted companies or businesses issuing shares
on the Alternative Investment Market (AIM), while an
EIS invests in a single company. In the current tax
year, 2006–07, income tax relief on VCTs is 30% and
on EIS investments it is 20%. The maximum
investment in a VCT is £200,000 per tax year while
up to £400,000 can go into an EIS. There is no tax to
pay on dividends or any profits you make on shares
held for a minimum of three years in an EIS, or five
years in a VCT.

The problem with these investments is that the
smaller, newer companies in which they invest are
the most likely to go bust. So you must only put in
these schemes money that you can afford to lose –
which means that despite their attractiveness from
a tax point of view they are not much good for most
people's retirement savings.

Non-tax-free retirement savings options
Investment funds. The most popular way to hold
investment funds is through stocks and shares ISAs,
but if you have used up your annual ISA allowance, it
is worth considering direct investment in unit trusts,
open-ended investment companies (OEICS) or
investment trusts. You can normally make regular
savings from £20 a month, or lump sum investments from £250. These funds offer a wide range

of investment choices, from specialist UK and overseas shares funds to bond funds and property funds. Global funds, which invest in stockmarkets all round the world, are a good choice for the long term if you are not sure exactly where to invest. Or if you have between five and ten years to go until retirement you could consider a stakeholder savings type fund, which invests in a mixture of shares and bonds or cash and has its annual charges capped at 1.5% (for more details see www.stakeholdersavings .gov.uk). Bonds and property funds are seen as lower-risk choices as you get closer to retirement, though they can also fluctuate in value.

Guaranteed equity bonds. These bonds are lump sum investments designed for investors who would like to invest in the stockmarket but don't want to lose any money. Usually offered by banks, building societies and insurance companies, they run for terms of between three and six years and your returns are linked to the performance of a stock-market index, often the FTSE 100 Index, which tracks the share price movements of the UK's largest 100 companies. If the index falls over the period you are guaranteed your capital back, though after inflation its buying-power will be less. Sometimes there is a minimum return on top regardless of what has happened to the stockmarket. If the stockmarket does rise over the period of your investment, you won't get as much as you would have done investing in an ordinary tracker fund because you won't receive any share dividends. Minimum investment starts at £1,000. Bear in mind also that it is not possible to withdraw money early from these bonds without penalty.

must know

Seeking financial advice

If you are unsure about where to invest before and after retirement, seek the advice of an independent financial adviser. See the Financial Services Authority's (FSA) factsheets: 'Choosing a financial adviser – how keyfacts can help you'; and the FSA guide to financial advice, available from the FSA's website www.fsa.gov.uk or tel: 0845 606 1234. There are a number of advisers and organisations that can give you names of independent financial advisers in your locality. IFA Promotion, www.unbiased.co.uk, tel: 0800 085 3250; Institute of Financial Planning, www.financialplanning. org.uk, tel: 0117 945 2470; and The Personal Finance Society, www.thepfs.org.

How to invest your savings when you reach retirement

Before retirement your main emphasis will be on building up your savings. When you get to retirement, you will need to rethink your investment strategy if you want your savings to generate some income to supplement your pension. You may also want to invest your tax-free lump sum so it gives you extra income.

To maximise your income at retirement you will need to make sure you pay as little tax on it as possible. If you are in a partnership, one way you may be able to save tax when you reach retirement is to make sure your savings are split between you to take full advantage of your personal tax allowances. For example, if all the savings are in one partner's name and that partner is a taxpayer while the other isn't, tax can be saved by transferring the savings into the non-taxpayer's name.

The main income investment options are as follows.

Cash

Security of capital is important when you retire so you will need to keep a greater proportion of your money in savings accounts than when you were working. Each tax year, make maximum use of your cash ISA allowance in order to shelter your interest from tax. If you need a regular income, seek out top-paying accounts that will transfer interest monthly into your bank account. Internet and postal accounts are often the most competitive. If you are a non-taxpayer remember to register for gross interest using form R85, available from your bank or building society.

If you are investing a large sum, it may be advisable to spread it around a number of banks and building societies. If one bank or building society fails (very rare in this day and age), the maximum compensation payable under the Financial Services Compensation Scheme is £31,700.

Mind the age allowance trap

When you get to age 65 your personal tax allowance will increase – from £5,035 to £7,280 in the tax year 2006-07. When you reach 75 it goes up further to £7,420. All the income you receive up to this amount will be tax free. The remainder will be taxed as normal.

However, if your income exceeds a certain level (£20,100 for 2006-07), your age allowance will be gradually reduced by £1 for every £2 that you are over the limit until it gets down to the same level as the normal personal allowance for the under 65s. In other words once your income exceeds £24,590 in the 2006-07 tax year if you are over 65 or £24,870 if you are over 75, you will be getting no extra tax allowance at all.

It is important to try and avoid your income falling between these levels because you will end up paying tax of 33% on this income. This is made up of the basic 22% tax due on each extra pound you receive over the limit, plus 11% due to the loss of age allowance.

Here are some ways you may be able to prevent your income exceeding the age allowance limit:
• If you are married or in a civil partnership, split income-producing savings between the two of you so you can claim two allowances.
• Choose investments that provide a tax-free income.
• If you have investments where the capital has grown in value, use some of these gains to supplement your income. Your annual capital gains tax allowance means you can take up to £8,800 (for the 2006-07 tax year) free of tax.
• Avoid cashing in insurance bonds/income bonds. The gains count as income for age allowance purposes.

National Savings and Investments Pensioners' Bonds

Backed by the Government, nothing can beat the security offered by National Savings and Investments. Pensioners' bonds have the added attraction that they will pay you a fixed monthly income over either a one-, two- or five-year term. Fixed-rate bank and building society accounts may pay higher rates but few pay interest monthly. You can invest between £500 and £1m in pensioners' bonds. Interest is paid gross but is liable to tax and must be declared to the taxman.

Guaranteed income bonds

These are another option if you want a regular fixed income. They are sold by insurance companies. Minimum investments normally start at £5,000 and they run for terms of between one and five years. Income is payable either monthly or half-yearly. These bonds are not suitable for non-taxpayers as basic rate tax is deducted at source and cannot be reclaimed. Basic rate taxpayers will have no further tax to pay on the income.

Individual Savings Accounts (ISAs)

ISAs are a very useful way of generating a tax-efficient income when you retire, and there is a good choice of income-focused investment funds available within stocks and shares ISAs. Current rules allow you to invest up to £7,000 per tax year in an ISA. This can be split: up to £3,000 can go into a mini-cash ISA and £4,000 into a stocks and shares ISA, or the whole £7,000 can go into a stocks and shares maxi ISA. If you have PEPs (Personal Equity

must know

Best ISAs

For details of best buy mini cash ISAs go to www.moneyfacts.co.uk or www.moneynet.co.uk.

Plans – the tax efficient savings plans which preceded ISAs) and ISAs that you have taken out in the past you can also switch them into income-producing funds without affecting their tax status.

Here are the main ISA income options:

1) Cash ISAs

If you are keen to minimise risk, the first thing you should do is make maximum use of your mini-cash ISA allowance. Look for the top-paying bank or building society account. The interest is tax free and usually competitive so you are likely to get a better return than you would from an ordinary savings account. Most cash ISAs pay out interest once a year but if you would like a more regular income, look for the small number which offer monthly interest payouts. For details of best-buy mini-cash ISAs go to www.moneyfacts.co.uk or www.moneynet.co.uk.

2) Stocks and shares ISAs

Bond funds: Bond funds can be a good investment for income seekers. Bonds are loans to governments and companies which pay a fixed rate of interest. The interest paid by the bonds generates a relatively high income which is tax-free for investors in ISAs. Bonds tend to fluctuate in value less than shares so your capital is regarded as relatively secure, although these funds are not without some risk and your investment can go down in value. The income can also fluctuate. It is usually paid out quarterly or half-yearly.

Equity income funds. Companies pay out their profits to shareholders in the form of regular dividends. Equity income funds invest in the shares of companies that pay a high and growing level of dividends. Returns on equity income funds usually

must know

Best equity funds

For information on top-performing equity income funds see the *Principal Income Study*, available from www.principalinvestment.co.uk or tel: 01225 460 010 start off lower than those on savings accounts but because dividends have historically grown over time they generally produce a better income in the medium to long term. The capital value of the funds has also increased in the past. Although past performance is no guide to the future, equity income funds have traditionally been a way of helping to protect your income and capital from inflation – an important consideration when you may be spending 20 to 30 years in retirement. For information on top-performing equity income funds see the Principal Income Study, available from www .principalinvestment.co.uk or tel: 01225 460 010.

Case study

Malcolm, 65, has recently retired. His total pension from his job and the state pension is nearly £17,000 a year. His wife Mary, 61, is also retired but she has no private pension and only receives a modest state pension of around £4,000 a year, which falls below her personal allowance of £5,035. They have some cash ISAs but Malcolm also has £20,000 in an ordinary building society account in his name. After he has paid tax on the interest, they receive £720 a year from it. Malcolm transfers the £20,000 into Mary's name so that she can put it against her personal allowance, so they now receive the £900 interest in full on these savings.

Distribution funds

If you are an income investor, it is a good idea to invest in a mixture of bond and equity income funds to spread your risk. This way you should get a reasonable income and some capital security but also have some prospect of income and capital growth. If you choose distribution funds, you generally get a mixture of both investments in one fund since they typically invest around 60% in bonds and 40% in equities.

Commercial property funds

The main attraction of investing in commercial property is the rental income it produces, so having a part of your investment in property funds makes sense if you are an income investor. In recent years these funds have also achieved considerable capital growth but after such a good run this is not expected to continue. Your capital should be relatively secure in a property fund but it could still go down in value.

Investment funds

When you have used up your annual ISA allowance you can still invest direct in any of the funds mentioned above. If you do this you can gradually move them into ISAs in future tax years to shelter them from tax. This will involve selling your holdings and buying them back again within an ISA, but if you use a fund supermarket via a discount broker, this will help reduce the cost.

Investment trusts are often more cost-effective if you invest in them outside an ISA. Many of the global and UK investment trusts have long histories of increasing their dividends year after year, and can be very attractive for income investors.

Investment bonds

Investment bonds are sold by life assurance companies. They offer a variety of investment funds within a single 'wrapper'. Most of the funds are stockmarket-linked and they can go down as well as up in value.

There are two arguments for putting money into investment bonds rather than directly into funds, but these are mainly relevant for higher-rate tax payers. The first is that you can withdraw 5% a year from your bond as income without having

must know

Care IFAs

To find an independent financial adviser who can advise on immediate care annuities go to www.IFAcare.co.uk or tel: 01562 822955.

to pay higher rate tax on these withdrawals at the time. You can go on making these withdrawals and defer any higher rate tax for up to 20 years or until you cash in your bond. (The insurance company itself pays tax, which covers your basic rate tax liability anyway.) The second argument is that you can move your money between different investment funds without having to pay any capital gains tax.

The reason bonds have these tax advantages is that they are a type of life insurance policy, although typically they only pay out around 1% extra on top of the value of your investment if you die. However, if you are a basic rate taxpayer you do not normally gain any income tax advantage since your liability is covered by the tax the insurance companies pays and you won't normally pay capital gains tax because most gains you get are likely to be covered by your annual capital gains tax allowance (£8,800 for the 2006–07 tax year).

Bonds pay more initial commission to financial advisers than investment funds when they are first sold, which may influence their recommendations. This does not actually make bonds more expensive providing they are held for at least 10 years, but it does mean that if you want your cash back in the first five years you will have to pay a penalty.

When income is needed to pay for care

If you need to pay for residential care for yourself or for an elderly relative, it is worth considering an annuity. Although most annuities – lump-sum, non-returnable investments that provide a guaranteed lifetime income – are bought to provide pensions, there is another type of annuity known as a 'purchased life annuity' that can be particularly useful for paying care-home fees. These annuities used to be a popular income investment in the days when there was little or no inflation, but nowadays few people buy them for this purpose.

If you are concerned about the potential long-term cost of residential care an 'immediate care fees annuity' can be a solution to this problem. These plans will pay a guaranteed tax-free amount, rising at a fixed rate of say 3% if required, for as long as you need care. The lump sum cost will depend on your state of health when you enter care, which will be assessed by the annuity company on the basis of medical evidence. The cost for someone who needs care due to a severe stroke is likely to be less than for someone who is suffering from dementia which has not affected their life expectancy.

While these annuities may not appear cheap, they provide peace of mind by putting a cap on the care costs and allow any remaining capital to be invested more productively elsewhere.

want to know more?

• *Which* is a respected quality-for-money checking organisation that publishes a monthly magazine and also has a useful website. They often run features on financial products that are worth checking out. Tel: 0845 307 4000, www.which.co.uk
• See also *Money Management* (020 8606 7545) and *Investment, Life and Pensions Moneyfacts* (0870 2250 100).
• Some good books on investment include: *Beginners Guide to Investment* by Bernard Gray; *The Sunday Times Money Guide*; *The Motley Fool UK Investment Guide*; and the *IC A-Z of Investment* by Caroline Sefton.

weblinks

• www.moneyfacts.co.uk
• www.moneyextra.com
• www.find.co.uk
• www.investmentgateway.com

Appendices

Glossary

Added years extra years you can buy to add to a salary-related pension to increase the amount you get on retirement.

Annuity an insurance product that you can buy at retirement to provide you with a guaranteed income for life.

Assets different types of investment such as shares or property

AVCs additional voluntary contributions – extra amounts you pay into a company-sponsored individual pension scheme to increase the pension you will get.

Blue-chip shares shares in large, well-established companies.

Bonds an investment in which you lend money to a company or to the government (gilts, q.v.) in return for interest payments and capital return.

Contracting out choosing to put your state second pension national insurance contributions into a personal pension scheme.

Diversification choosing different types of investments from a variety of sources so that you don't have all your eggs in one basket.

Equities shares in a company. When you buy an equity (or a share) you own a small part of the company concerned.

Equity release a scheme that lets you borrow money against the value of your home while continuing to live there.

FTSE a company owned by the Financial Times and the London Stock Exchange, which measures share price movements.

Funds where money from individual savers is pooled together to buy large numbers of shares or other investments such as property.

Gilts investments where you lend money to the government in return for fixed interest payments and a return of capital after a fixed period.

Group personal pension a group of individual pensions run by a pension provider to which the employee and employer both contribute.

Home Responsibilities Protection a scheme whereby those who have been out of the workforce because they have been caring for dependants can maintain their state pension rights.

IFA an independent financial adviser, who can give advice on all financial products on offer rather than being tied to a few individual companies.

Income drawdown taking some income from your pension fund without turning it into an annuity.

Inflation rising prices. The

rate at which they rise each year is known as the rate of inflation.

ISA an individual savings account in which you can invest a limited amount of money each year and get tax-free returns.

Life insurance an insurance policy that will provide for your dependants if you die while the policy is still running.

Lifestyle fund a fund designed to change its investment from higher-earning, higher-risk ones when you are younger, to lower-risk ones as you approach retirement.

Money-purchase pension a pension scheme in which you build up a lump sum with which you can buy an annuity (q.v.) on retirement.

National Savings and Investments a range of savings products backed by the government.

Occupational pensions pension schemes of different types set up by employers for their employees.

Open market option your right to buy an annuity (q.v.) from any company you want.

Pension credits state top-ups for pensioners whose income falls below a set level.

Personal pension a pension open to everyone which may not be as low cost as a stakeholder pension (q.v.) but may offer more investment choice.

S2P the state second pension, since 2002, which is related to earnings.

Salary-related pension a pension scheme in which your employer guarantees to pay you a percentage of your average or final salary for the rest of your life.

SERPS the state earnings-related pension scheme that ran from 1978 to 2002.

SIPPs self-invested personal pensions, for those who want to put their retirement savings into a wider range of investments.

Stakeholder pensions low-cost, flexible pension schemes open to everyone.

State retirement pension the basic pension paid by the government, which depends on the amount of national insurance contributions you have made during your working life.

Tax relief money back from the government. If you pay basic rate tax, each £1 that goes into your pension fund includes 22p tax relief so it only costs you 78p.

Tracker fund an investment product designed to follow the movement of a given share index, such as the FTSE 100.

Transfer value if you want to leave one pension scheme and take your money to another, this is the amount you will be allowed to transfer.

Trustees people who look after pension schemes on behalf of savers.

Venture Capital Trust a risky type of investment in which you back small businesses.

Further reading

Free leaflets are available on a range of pension topics from several organisations.

The Pension Service

Part of the Department of Work and Pensions (DWP)

Tel: 0845 731 3233 www.thepension service.gov.uk

- A guide to your pension options (PM1)
- State pensions – your guide (PM2)
- Occupational pensions – your guide (PM3)
- Personal pensions – your guide (PM4)
- Pensions for the self-employed – your guide (PM5)
- Pensions for women – your guide (PM6)
- Contracted-out pensions – your guide (PM7)
- Stakeholder pensions – your guide (PM8)
- State pensions for parents and carers – your guide (PM9)
- Important information for married people – Inheritance of SERPS (SERPSL1)
- Pension credit – at a glance (PCO9S)
- A guide to pension credit (PC1L)
- Understanding your state pension forecast (BR19L)
- State pension – the choices available to you (BR33)
- Your pension statement (CPF5)

- State pension – the choices available to customers living overseas (IPC327C)
- Your guide to state pension deferral (SPD1)

The Financial Services Authority (FSA)

Tel: 0845 606 1234 www.fsa.gov.uk

FSA guides:

- FSA Guide to Pensions 1: Starting a pension
- FSA Guide to Pensions 2: Reviewing your pensions
- FSA Guide to Pensions 3: Annuities and income withdrawal
- FSA Guide to financial advice
- FSA Guide to making a complaint about financial services
- FSA Guide to the risks of salary-related occupational pension transfers

FSA factsheets:

- The State Second Pension and contracting out
- Income Withdrawal – Pension changes
- Income Withdrawal – a retirement option for you?
- Retiring Soon – What you need to do about your pensions

- Stakeholder Pensions and Decision Trees
- Important Information About Your Yearly Pension Statement
- Unlocking Pensions – Make sure you understand the risks
- Raising Money From Your Home

HM Revenue & Customs (HMRC)

Tel: 0115 974 1670 www.hmrc.gov.uk
- IR3: Personal Pension Schemes (including Stakeholder Pension Schemes) – a guide for members of tax approved schemes
- IR2: Occupational Pension Schemes – a guide for members of tax-approved schemes.
- IR121: Income tax and pensioners
- IR138: Living or retiring abroad – a guide to UK tax on your UK income and pension
- CA5603: Voluntary NI Contributions

The Pension Protection Fund

Tel: 0845 600 2541 www.pension protectionfund.org.uk
- An Introductory Guide to the Pension Protection Fund

The Pensions Advisory Service

Tel: 0845 601 2923 www.opas.org.uk
- Concerned about your pension?
- Getting information about your pension

- Ill-health early retirement
- The Pensions Advisory Service and the Pensions Ombudsman
- Pension Dispute Procedure
- Personal Pension Problems
- Transferring your pension to another scheme
- What are Additional Voluntary Contributions
- Where is my pension?
- Winding up a pension scheme
- Women and pensions

Magazines

Money Management
FT Business
Tabernacle Court
16–28 Tabernacle Street
London EC2A 4DD
Tel: 020 8606 7545

Moneyfacts
Moneyfacts House
66–70 Thorpe Road
Norwich NR1 1BJ
Tel: 0870 2250 100
www.moneyfacts.co.uk

Which?
Castlemead
Gascoyne Way
Hertford SG14 1LH
Tel: 0845 307 4000
www.which.co.uk

Useful addresses

Official bodies

Financial Services Authority
25 The North Colonnade
Canary Wharf
London E14 5HS
Tel: 0845 606 1234
www.fsa.gov.uk

Financial Ombudsman Service
South Quay Plaza
183 March Wall
London E14 9SR
Tel: 0845 080 1800
www.financial-ombuds
man.org.uk

Pensions Advisory Service
11 Belgrave Road
London SW1V 1RB
Tel: 0845 601 2923
www.opas.org.uk

Pensions Ombudsman
11 Belgrave Road
London SW1V 1RB
Tel: 020 7834 9144
www.pensions-ombuds
man.org.uk

The Pensions Regulator
Napier House
Trafalgar Place
Brighton BN1 4DW
Tel: 0870 606 3636
www.thepensionsregulator
.gov.uk

Pension Protection Fund
Knollys House
17 Addiscombe Road
Croydon
Surrey CR0 6SR
Tel: 0845 6002541
www.pensionprotection
fund.org.uk

Financial Services Compensation Scheme
7th Floor, Lloyds Chambers
Portsoken Street,
London E1 8BN
Tel 7892 7300
www.fscs.org.uk

The Pension Service
Contact your local DWP
office or Jobcentre
Tel: 0845 606 0265
www.thepensionservice
.gov.uk

State Pension Forecasting Team
Future Pension Centre
The Pension Service
Tyneview Park
Whitley Road
Newcastle upon Tyne
NE98 1BA
Tel: 0845 300 0168
www.thepensionservice.gov.u

Pension Tracing Service
The Pension Service
Tyneview Park
Whitley Road
Newcastle upon Tyne
NE98 1BA
Tel: 0845 600 2537
www.thepensionservice.gov.u

HM Revenue and Customs
Your local tax office or any HM
Revenue and Customs Enquiry
Centre
www.hmrc.gov.uk

Financial advisors

IFA Promotion
117 Farringdon Road
London EC1R 3BX
Tel: 0800 085 3250
www.unbiased.co.uk

**Institute of Financial
Planning**
Whitefriars Centre
Lewins Mead
Bristol BS1 2NT
Tel: 0117 945 2470
www.financialplanning
.org.uk

**The Personal Finance
Society**
42-48 High Road
London E18 2JP
Tel: 020 8530 0852
www.thepfs.org

Specialist annuity advisors

Annuity Direct
32 Scrutton Street
London EC2A 4RQ
Tel: 0500 506 575
www.annuitydirect.co.uk

The Annuity Bureau
Alexander Forbes House
6 Bevis Marks
London EC3A 7AF
Tel: 0845 602 6263
www.annuity-bureau.co.uk

**William Burrows
Annuities**
Northumberland House
303-306 High Holborn
London WC1V 7JZ
www.williamburrows.com

Equity release

**Safe Home Income Plans
(SHIP)**
PO Box 516
Preston Central PR2 2XQ
Tel: 0870 241 6060
www.ship-ltd.org

Age Concern
Astral House
1268 London Road
London SW16 4ER
Tel 0800 009 966
www.ace.org.uk

Help the Aged
207-221 Pentonville Road
London N1 9UZ
Tel: 0808 800 6565
www.helptheaged.co.uk

Index